AS TALL AS MY HEART

A Mother's Measure of Love

♥♥♥♥♥♥♥♥ ♥♥♥♥♥♥ ♥♥
MARJORIE HOLMES
♥♥♥♥♥♥♥♥♥♥♥♥♥♥♥

Of the thousands of moving prayers and essays Marjorie Holmes has written, none has ever evoked more response from her readers than "How Tall Am I, Mother?" The answer, AS TALL AS MY HEART, became the title of this book not only because of the popularity of the piece but because it sets the theme for all of these selections. Like songs of joy, they give voice to the depth and breadth and ever-presence of a mother's love. Whether Marjorie Holmes writes of the loss of a first tooth, the litany of a homework drill, a visit to a zoo or train station, the shared, quiet joy of a night under the stars, or a child's spontaneous prayer of thankfulness, she affirms what all mothers know: "No matter how tall and strong he may become, or what heights he may attain—no child ever grows beyond the reach of his mother's heart."

BOOKS BY MARJORIE HOLMES

AS TALL AS
MY HEART

A MOTHER'S MEASURE OF LOVE

Marjorie Holmes

A Love and Laughter Book
EPM Publications, Inc.
McLean, Virginia, 1974

Distributed by Hawthorn Books

ISBN: 0-914440-03-9
Library of Congress Catalog Card Number: 74-75733

To Mother

Acknowledgment

The author wishes to thank the Washington *Star* for permission to include *HOW TALL AM I, MOTHER?* and other material from her *Love and Laughter* column.

TABLE OF CONTENTS

HOW TALL AM I, MOTHER?

How tall am I? Let me measure!" the children are always saying. And they run to fling themselves into your arms, and then to stand straight and tall, straining, straining.

How little they are at first. But you say, "My, how big! Why, you're up to my knees." Then, "Up to my hips." Or—"Why, honey, you're up to my ribs."

"Am I up to your heart yet?" one of them will ask. "How soon will I be up to your heart?"

"Next year maybe, or sooner if you drink your milk," you say. "Hurry up now. Hurry."

Then at last the day arrives. The round, firm shining head that is pressed against you is there—up to your very heart.

"I'm here!" the child exclaims. "I'm tall enough to hear it pounding. I'm up to your heart now—I'm big!" he cries.

But children don't stop growing. Soon, only too soon, they are up to your chin. And the heart that has been their measure begins to protest: "Oh, no. Slow down. Wait, don't grow so fast!"

But there is no waiting. On they go, up and up, until one day they are gazing at you levelly, eye to eye. And then soon, all too soon, to your dismay, they have outstripped you. They are above you, gazing down.

"Remember," they ask sometimes in a fond, triumphant amusement, "how I used to want to be as tall as your heart?"

"Yes, wasn't that funny?" you laugh. And think: *AS TALL AS MY HEART.* Up to my heart, and then shooting so far beyond it. Or so they believe. And you wouldn't diminish their pleasure for the world.

But you know—and this is your secret: That no matter how tall and strong he may become, or what heights he may attain— no child ever really grows beyond the reach of his mother's heart.

PARENTHOOD IS NOW!

Parenthood is—now. The good of it and the bad of it are immediate, this moment.

It's in piling children into a station wagon and driving them to the zoo. It's in staying up late to sew on CubScout badges. It's in coaching them for exams and trotting anxiously to the school when they fail. It's in getting up at night to see that they're dry and warm, or that they take that vital medicine every 4 hours. It's in sustaining them through the heart's worse illnesses, when a daughter keeps anguished vigil by the telephone praying for a call that doesn't come. It's in getting them ready for plays and dance recitals and to Sunday School on time.

It's in these tasks, these burdens, these blessed if exhausting duties which you think sometimes you can bear no longer, yet know of course that you can, you will—and which you know you'll miss, feel actually bereft of, when they're over.

And the rewards, like the strains of parenthood, are *now*.

Not in some rosy future when your children will be grown and presumably do you honor by gifts and phone calls and little attentions, and above all by warm memories of what superb parents you were.

Let's not kid ourselves about that. They won't! They'll be too busy with their own offspring.

Their time and attention and concern will be devoted to their own activities and responsibilities— getting up at night with medicine and piling the station wagon full and praying that Mary will get that date to the dance and herding their own flock off to plays and dancing recitals and Sunday School.

If they think of you at all it will be with a nagging sense of obligation. "Oh, dear, I really should write home." Or, "Heavens, it can't be Dad's birthday already—and he's so hard to buy for, too."

As for those glowing tributes as to what marvelous parents you were—! No, no, let's face it, far more often it is, unfairly, the mistakes our parents made that we remember, the frailties, the errors. And it's an undeniable part of growing up that once sons and daughters become adults they feel entitled to talk back, criticize.

You did. And yours will too.

So the real rewards of parenthood are found not over some peaceful hill when one by one the responsibilities have flown. They are here as close as the baby's crib. . . as a son bending over his homework . . . as a daughter singing in the shower.

Parenthood is now!

THE SECRET WORLD

A mother and her newborn child live in a secret world, a small enchanted realm of their own. Brightly over its rim peer the faces of others. The father. The brothers and sisters. The grandparents and aunts and eager, interested friends. Yet despite their nearness and their love they are aliens, outside the mystic gates.

To the mother in these first enthralled days at least, the only reality is the round pink shapeless unwritten-on face of the miracle she has created. The hot light weight of the blanketed flesh she cradles in her arms. The frail thrilling scent of him, so delicate yet so definite in its power to stir her. The raw sweet sound of his cries.

Together they are the universe, these two, sufficient unto each other, physically and emotionally linked in a way no relationship can ever equal again.

And yet out of this nest of joy, this ecstatic union, the mother feels herself rising on tides of tenderness for those outside. Feeling perhaps a bit guilty in her complete absorption, she reaches out to them urging, "Oh, come in, come in!"

Love flows out of her, like waves too strong to be contained. Her husband is dearer than before, in an exciting new way. And the others too take on a delightful new significance—for are they not admirers of her magical gift to the world? Are they not its friends, its kin? Soon she will return to them and resume her former role; soon this helpless precious newcomer will be introduced to his role—as just another person, another member of the family.

Meanwhile, the wonder . . . meanwhile, their private dream.

♥ ♥ ♥

SOME OF THE NICEST FEELINGS
IN THE WORLD

A baby curled kittenlike over your shoulder, fast asleep. . .
A little child's hand trustingly clasped in yours.

BABY VIKING

The snow is beginning to melt. The sun floods everything with a dazzling brilliance. It capers and leaps along the creek. It twinkles on the snow crustings. The air smells of spring.

You bundle the baby into his blue snowsuit and peaked cap, and wearing slacks and boots and brief bright coat, lead him along beside you to the corner mailbox.

He shuffles experimentally along in his stubby galoshes. He teeters and wobbles on the walks that are rough and snow-crusted. He runs, in his fat, eager waddle, whenever he comes to a shoveled space. He aims unerringly for every puddle, blissfully sloshing through with an air of delighted discovery.

You do not try to restrain him; his shining eyes, his ecstatic chuckle are pleasures too eloquent to resist.

He kicks out at snowy banks. He shrieks with glee when you throw snowballs at him, and squats at once to grab at the white stuff with his own awkward mittened hands and tries to hurl it back. His cheeks become two scarlet balloons. His nose runs joyously. Enhanced by the snowy sunlight, his eyes are round and full and shining like immense blue marbles.

He is a fat little Viking, a king's son, a ruddy Norseman who belongs in the cold Northland. And when you unbundle him, peeling him down like a bulb for the warmth inside, he too has the fresh sweet melting scent of the coming spring.

♥ ♥ ♥

FOR A CHILD JUST LEARNING
TO TALK

Enrapt, he watches the wondrous ways
Of other lips fashioning speech.
With all of his being, the wakening mind,
The eager heart, even the arms, you feel him reach
Out for this magical tool,
Drawing it to himself with shining eyes,
Tasting it, testing it, rolling it on his tongue,
The lovely pebbles of sound,
The bright web flung
About all human creatures.
Amusing are his tries to speak, to tell.
Yet sometimes they dim the eyes as well.

ATTABOY, GOD!

Evening, and a light snow beginning to fall . . . The children press their noses excitedly to the window, urging the frail flakes on.

The snowflakes are tentative, only a pale glinting in the kitchen light. Like fireflies darting, or lost spirits seeking a way to go. A few settle, cling to a twig or lightly dust the ground.

"Will there be enough for a snowman? Can we go sledding tomorrow?"

"I doubt it. Come on now, bedtime."

You lead them reluctantly toward baths. By the time the commotion of hurled towels and missing pajamas and who gets which story is settled, they've forgotten . . . Except for the four-year-old. Piling out of bed, he darts to the window, struggles back the curtains, and emits a joyful shout:

"It's snowing, it's really showing! . . . *Attaboy, God!*"

The fervor, the joy, the awe. The sheer exultation, bringing others spilling from their nests to gaze upon this wonder, the now swiftly falling snow. This white explosion, this whirling, sparkling stardust that will change their world by morning. What a marvel . . . And surely no prayer of praise and thanksgiving was ever uttered with more enthusiasm than that simple outburst.

God is so close to children, so real, if you simply provide the name for that which they instinctively feel. Fresh from their own Creator, they sense His closeness. "Where did I come from?" they ask. But deep inside they already know. Physically they come from us, their parents—this we must explain. But the secret of their own beginnings in the very source of life itself, they understand in a way that surpasses words. In a way more intensely pure and certain than it will ever be again.

Children's prayers are in their eyes, rejoicing over a bird or a butterfly, a stone, a bug, a flower. In the arms they fling blissfully to embrace the wind or rain or falling snow. In the bodies they hurl with such abandon into tall grass or rolling and tumbling down a sunny hill. Children love the Author of their universe, and their first prayers, once they know His name, are almost any spontaneous version of "Attaboy, God!"

Should we bother then about "teaching" them how to "pray"? Yes, I think we should. Bedtime prayers, and blessings at meals, prayers in little rhymes and chants, prayers to learn and remember as well as prayers of their own. Children have an almost pathetic eagerness to be so equipped. There is something forlorn about putting a child to bed who's never said his prayers.

"Kneel down? What *for?*" His face lights up as you explain. He joins the others, mimics the folded hands, peeks around for guidance. Is this just to be like friends or cousins? I don't think so. Children want adults to care enough about them to teach them such things. They want to be taught ways to worship just as they want to be taught how to fish or swim or ride a bicycle or play the piano. We can foster their natural yearning to communicate with their Maker, we can direct. The Lord's Prayer, the Twenty Third

Psalm, a rich heritage of hymn and Bible song and story—they have a right to these treasures, and we ought to be as concerned that they get them as we are that they get their spelling or multiplication tables.

True, with time and repetition prayers can lose significance. Too often we just "rattle them off" without thinking, and people say they don't do any good. (This was said, for instance, to justify depriving children of prayers at school.) Well, we also eat food without thinking, too preoccupied to taste it, but that doesn't mean it doesn't nourish us. . . . Prayer nourishes the spirit. Any prayers, the most familiar, most ritual—their truths deeply etch the subconscious, their phrases have a way of soaring to the surface when we least expect. In times of loneliness or loss or fear or need; in times of happiness too great to contain:

> Though I walk through the valley of the
> shadow of death I will fear no evil . . . Forgive
> us our trespasses as we forgive . . . In Thy
> presence is fullness of joy . . . The peace of
> God which passeth all understanding . . .

How much poorer our lives would be without the prayers our parents taught us. How much we can teach our children in return . . . And how much we can learn from them.

"Attaboy, God!"

Dignified? No. Not even time for such a grownup concept as respect. But such genuine joy. Such fervent praise. Such absolute acceptance of the nature of God and His power to bestow.

We are so wordy, we adults. So self-conscious, so cluttered with protests and worries, and we can make religion so complex. We need to become again like

11

little children shouting our welcome to wonders almost too marvelous to believe. Whirling snow. A flower that grows and bursts from a tiny seed. . . . This magical world and our lives upon it. How incredible, how glorious!

We ought to leap from our sluggish beds, from the blind sleep of taking for granted, and rush to the windows of life. Rejoicing. Applauding. Praising. Calling out with every cell of our beings: "Attaboy, God!"

THE FIRST LOOSE TOOTH

At long last, after months of watching other kids shed theirs, your little boy discovers a tooth is loose.

"Look, look!" He bares it in gleeful grimace. With vast and cautious pride, he inserts a grubby finger and demonstrates. He emits an eloquent sigh. "I can hardly believe it!"

But when you say, "Let's pull it," he beats a fast retreat. "Oh, no, I've got to wiggle it a while. Hey, let's call Daddy up and tell him."

"Aaah, what's so great about a loose tooth?" the Voice of Experience derides. "Lookit me—" A hideous gap is exposed. "Lookit how many I lost already."

"You're older. Hey, kids, look!"

It is a source of attention the rest of the afternoon. You catch him blissfully wiggling it in rare repose. And when his father drives up, he streaks to the car with the news.

"Okay, great, let's pull it. Would you prefer the pliers, or tying a string to the knob and slamming the door?"

He blanches. "Well–l–l—I would like to show the kids at school."

"That's right," you remind his father in undertones. "He is awfully late at losing them. Let him enjoy it a while."

Your husband grins, suspecting the foolish secret reluctance you feel. Mothers! Clinging. Postponing, if only for a day, so small a milestone in a son's maturing as pulling a baby tooth.

You watch the star of this little drama trudge off the next day, still importantly wiggling. To your surprise, it's still intact, though hanging by a thread, when he comes home at noon.

"Honey, I do think we ought to get it out of there. Let me feel—"

"No, no, no; you might jerk."

"Pull it, pull it!" brothers and sisters yell. "Don't be such a baby."

"You'll get some money if you do. The good fairy'll leave a dime under your pillow."

"Heck, I get a quarter. But when he's my age—"

He is backing into a corner, hand protective over his mouth. His eyes are suddenly big with surprise. He emits a somewhat spitty yell. "It's out, it's out." He races for the bathroom, grabs a glass of water, proud of the blood he is shedding, prouder still of the contents of his clenched fist.

"You keep it for me, Mother, don't lose it." With great care he delivers it up.

It lies in your palm, tiny and jagged, almost rootless. The first bit of himself he must part with, you think. The first proud, pained severing.

NEVER NEVER LAND

There is a bare rutted place near the garage, and your son and a playmate have claimed it for their own.

For days on end they will squat there or trudge about, planning, contriving, surveying, or studying their "blueprints" (a piece of blue shirtboard on which they have chalked mystical convolutions) arguing with all the fierce intensity of engineers erecting the Aswan Dam.

"Let's make it go this way, farther to the right, and have the ships come in."

"You're crazy, man, that'll flood our landing field!"

Sometimes their disagreements are so mighty they almost come to war. Or one of them will fling down his shovel or the hose with which they've been filling the channels and stamp on home. But mostly they merge into a little unit of brown sweating backs and grubby shorts and towheads, and voices uttering the mystical chants of their enterprise: "Chug-chug-chug, here comes the barge—" "Rrrrr-eeee—bam! Watch out for that bulldozer—"

There is mud and mess and glint of metal as the sun pours down on toys and boys and all the clutter of improvised fleets and planes of sticks and stones. Bees drone in the lilacs nearby; squirrels scurry across the shining roof of the garage. Dogs come sniffing up and are embraced or shooed away as the mood demands. "Lookout, get 'im outta here, he'll

15

wreck the launching pad!"

Your husband, seeking a spot for a strawberry patch, announces, "I think I've got it—out there by the garage. It's an awful mess with all those ruts and junk, and the space is just going to waste."

He can't understand the vigor with which you protest: "Going to waste? You don't know what you're saying. That's a goldmine, an airport, a battleground, the site of the mightiest dam in the universe, the place where astronauts have been launched to the moon. You just can't plant strawberries in Never Never Land!"

♥ ♥ ♥

DOMESTIC DIALOGUE

Father: "No, honey, you can't take the baby turtle home to raise. His mommy would feel bad. What would your mommy say if somebody carried you away?"

Mother: "Hooray! Take his brothers and sisters too."

LITTLE BROTHER AND BIG DOLLS

The middle girl is busy about her dolls. You are aware of the scrape of chairs, a contented voice in one-sided murmurous conversation. "Now sit right here and be good. How would you like to be next to Shirley Temple? Oh, you poor thing, you need some new clothes."

Out of chairs and blankets and make-believe she has fashioned a kind of castle. Or a tented apartment house, its cubicles occupied by these smiling, inert personalities: A fat beaming baby doll, arms outstretched. Barbie dolls in poses of stiff sophistication, next door to a dangling, battered Raggedy Andy with dolls spilling all over his lap. At the very top perches a ballerina.

"She's the fairy queen," you are informed as she indicates the tiny stick wand, the star in the hair.

"It's lovely," you say, while little doors flick open along the corridors of time and you remember. . . you remember. . . "It's a wonderful doll temple. Oh-oh, here comes trouble."

For little brother has awakened from his nap and comes toddling, a gleam in his eye. "Me help, me help!"

"Help is right! Help! Take him away!"

You snatch up the frantically wiggling figure. But the architect weakens at his cries. "Oh, well, let him stay—which house do you want, honey?"

With swift determination, he climbs the nonesuch tower, grabs the "queen" and hugs her passionately

17

to his breast. Then with surprising placidity, he hands her over, yawns, and sits regarding the mysterious goings-on. His cheeks are as red as the rosiest doll's, his eyes as round, his legs in the corduroy trousers as chubby. In a moment he scrambles down.

Now what? You wonder, as he trudges to the bathroom, returning with comb and brush.

"Me help," he announces, taking the baby doll from its perch and sitting down. Earnestly he removes its ruffled bonnet and begins to comb and brush the shiny painted head.

Big sister regards him benignly and giggles. She tosses you a conspiratorial glance. "Little brothers!"

♥ ♥ ♥

THE SMALL FRY SAY

Four year old: "When I grow up I want to be a dancer and a mother and a plumber. And I want to marry Daddy and you can be the maid."

IT TAKES SO LITTLE TO PLEASE
A CHILD

It takes so little, so very little, to please a child.

We complain about the competition of television, deplore the plethora of sophisticated, over-realistic toys. Yet even as we provide them we notice that for the child himself nothing can destroy his own instinctive joy in simple things.

Such as: Swinging on doors... Climbing into cardboard cartons and scrooching down to hide... Dialing the time or the weather... Cutting pictures from a magazine...

Skipping rope, chasing a butterfly, throwing stones... Helping mother roll out pie dough or daddy build a birdhouse... Hunting four-leaf clovers... Curling up on somebody's lap or at his knee and listening to a story.

Sometimes when we hear ourselves contrasting the simple pleasures of our own childhood with the way things are today ("We made our own wooden airplanes, we drew our paper dolls—") let's pause to remember: It's only the adults who change; children will always be the same.

How long has it been since you've turned off the TV set or resisted the impulse to provide another super-toy, and said: "Let's go for a walk... Let's bake some cookies... Let's read a story."

♥ ♥ ♥

THINGS ONLY A MOTHER
WOULD EXPECT

The little boy spied, in the dimestore, a glittering 25 cent pin, which seemed to him the prettiest one in the world. Trying to suppress his excitement, he urged his mother to go on shopping down the street. Then, scrambling through his purse, he produced a quarter, and summoned a clerk.

"Gift wrap this, please," he ordered.

Off he trotted, proudly clutching his purchase—to find his mother gazing into the window of a jewelry store—upon an array of fine costume pins.

Pressing his face to the glass, he exclaimed, "Wow! How much does that big blue pin cost?"

"Forty-five dollars," she told him.

Staggered, he tried to take this in. Then, with a great sigh of triumph: "But wait'll you see the pin I bought you. It's not quite as big and shiny, but every bit as pretty. Why, gee— on you, Mom, it'll look like it might even cost a dollar!"

HER HEART IN HER EYES

A mother watches from windows. And her heart is in her eyes. . .

Her baby is sleeping in a carriage on the porch. She pauses in her work to look out. Is he covered? Is the hood tilted so the sun won't shine in his eyes? Is he safe, is he all right?

And running softly beneath this practical concern is the voice that sings its little song of wonder: "He is there—and he is mine!". . .

Her children go trooping off to school. Waving, she stands in the doorway, mentally checking: Did I remember to put the cookies in Susan's lunchbox? Will Freddy be warm enough in that sweater? Oh, why didn't I go through the times tables once more with Anne?

The door closes, she returns to her dishes. But as the bus pulls up, she darts to the window for one last glimpse. Her heart has propelled her— and her heart is in her eyes. . .

Her little girl bubbles down the walk toward a party, clutching the birthday present under her arm. "Goodbye, darling, be sure to tell them you had a nice time," she calls.

A son, combed and scrubbed, trudges off toward his first big date. To watch from the door would be too obvious, but she slips to the window, pulls back the curtain. "Oh, please let the girl be sweet and gay and good," she thinks. "And let him not be too shy, let him have a wonderful time." A helpless love goes out to him as she follows him with her eyes. . .

They are playing in the yard, the rough and tumble lot of them. Small daughters tagging each other, boys in a frenzy of football or leaf fights.

She darts, for no good reason, to the window, just to catch the bright commotion. And there is a twist of laughter in the voice that reminds her: "What noisy nuisances they are. But they're healthy, happy kids (and by golly, they are mine!)"

Or they give her hasty kisses as they rush off, all dressed up for Sunday School. . . She sees their uniformed backs departing for Cub meetings, or Brownies, or Boy Scout camp. . . Proudly carrying their bulging suitcases, they leave for weekend visits, or excitedly join the class for a senior trip. . .

Or they're waving from the bus that will carry them to college. . . Or, in a shower of rice, on the arm of a stranger, she sees her child being spirited away toward its own mysterious future. Disappearing that fateful, final time.

And no matter where they are going, or what they are doing, a mother's eyes keep watch. While somewhere within, the song continues: "These are bits of myself that I have created. There they go, and I wouldn't stop them—"

But her heart is in her eyes.

THE ZOO, A CHILD'S PARADISE

The zoo!" the children cry ever so often. "Oh, come on, let's all take a trip to the zoo." Its fascination never fails them, no matter how often they go. For there is something about animals that lures these small animals of our own. A purity and freedom and total lack of manners with which children can identify. Animals are so uninhibited, so absolute, so uncomplex. When animals feel like yelling they yell, when they feel like sleeping they sleep. Animals are forever free to rattle bars or make faces at people, or throw their food. Nobody spanks them (except for an occasional monkey mother); nobody says "Don't!"

And animals, particularly zoo animals, bring all the pungent flavor and thrill and mystery of far places to your door.

Here loom the huge, majestic, wrinkled gray elephants from India or Ceylon, their great trunks swaying. There lie the tawny lions from Africa. Giraffes regard you almost pathetically from the heights of those slender heads that might otherwise be cropping leaves from a palm tree south of the Sahara. While behind fences wander creatures curious, if less dramatic—the ibex, the zebra, the caribou.

As for the reptiles, they're always first choice. Nothing in the animal world is repellent to children: Children thrill to the cobras and the constrictors and the great ugly, lazy crocodiles.

They love the zoo with its raw, acidic smells, its

23

echoing screeches and spine-tingling roars. They envy the uniformed attendants moving so intimately about among these beasts, calling them chummily by name as they clean the cages, or shovel in food.

Flying their balloons, those signals of triumph over reluctant parents, munching popcorn or cotton candy, the children dart along the paths of their special paradise.

And pushing or carrying smaller brothers and sisters, the parents trudge after—all unaware that their own faces reflect delight too.

For the eternal child that lives in all of us has been awakened. It shines from our own eyes as we stand marveling before the flamingos, or awed before the leopards, or laughing at the antics of the polar bears. Most of us never outgrow it—the never-ending wonder and thrill of the zoo.

ENOUGH STARS TO GO AROUND

It's good to be a woman when . . .

Your husband suggests, "Let's sit on the patio and watch the stars. They look different tonight."

As they do. Instead of peppering the sky in their usual profusion, they climb its infinite reaches like ladders of light. The very constellations have assumed a new position, leading the eye up and up these diamond-studded stairs. The milky way is a plume of silver smoke.

The children, bound for bed, come spilling down to join you, trailing blankets, and you all huddle and cuddle together, remarking the thrilling mystery of the heavens.

"Just think, maybe the people on Mars are looking down at us right now wondering what we're like."

"Not down, stupid, they'd be looking up too. Besides, you can't tell from the pictures whether there's life there yet."

"There will be when we get there. Only I'm heading for the moon first, man. It's closer to home, easier to get back."

"What makes you think you're going?" . . . "Oh, I'm going, all right." They speak of space travel with the excited confidence with which people once watched ships set forth across uncharted seas, or the first airplane wing daringly off from a pasture.

"I think I'll visit that big green star over there first," the little one announces. "What's its name? It's my star, it winked at me."

"That's Jupiter," an older one advises importantly. "And it's not green and it didn't wink at you, you just think so. Besides, it's not yours."

"It is too my star if I want it, isn't it, Daddy?"

"Okay, sure, take any star you want."

"I choose that one!" another voice pipes up. "That big white one."

"No, no, that's my star, I saw it first!"

"For heaven's sake, don't fight," you laugh. "There are plenty of stars to go around."

MEMORY PICTURES...

Your toddler trying to lick chocolate from his face, kitty-fashion, with his tongue.

A freckled sixth-grader and his pigtailed sweetheart visiting ardently over the lunch table as to which of their friends loves whom —with circles of milk on their mouths...

Little boys peering impishly in the window, to the anguish and despair of their teenage sister, who's trying to teach a boy friend a new dance step...

Your first-grader bringing the cool sweetness of all outdoors inside as he bangs in at three. His nose is cold to your cheek, his eyes aglow as he describes the dramatic events of his world: "We had these movies at school, all about Indians, boy, and they're going to have a program, and if I sing real good they might choose me!"

DON'T HURRY!

Your husband gulps his coffee, paws his pockets for change (milk money, lunch money, allowances), and with hard male kisses for all, lopes out the door. "Hey, wait for me!" a tall son hollers, grabbing his jacket and galloping after to ride to school.

A daughter finishes her egg and springs up, a finger in the book that has been propped beside her plate. She flashes upstairs, and after half a dozen pleas, "How do I look? Is this sweater all right? Have I got enough lipstick on?", ties a bright bandana about her hair, flings a purse across her shoulders, and bangs out to greet her friends.

A boy who has been chasing the baby in some wild shrieking game, must be driven back to the table to finish. He reluctantly swallows the last of his tomato juice, his face emerging from the glass with upjutting red mustaches. Wiping his mouth on his hand, he tramps off for final toiletry.

"Bye," he grins, making a final lunge at the baby. "I'll bring home two gold stars today," he promises fervently, with a final hug. And the door bangs; he is poking off down the walk, the top of his head just showing above the hedge. You stand at the window holding the baby who watches intently, waving and waving until brother is out of sight.

You turn, and the wildly tumbled house confronts you. The loveseat piled with discarded mittens, sweaters, a baseball bat. Papers on the floor. The kitchen a hurricane of milk cartons, cereal boxes, eggshells, skillets. But your home is quiet now. There is a cheery gentleness about the very disorder, a silent sense of waiting.

You think, at first urgently, then with calm satisfaction of the day's many tasks—for after all, you can take your time. Your house is your kingdom and your domain, you can do things in the order and the manner that you choose. In a burst of gratefulness you hug the little one tighter. "Hi. Well, here we are alone again, you and I. Now where do we start?"

He cocks a blond silken head flirtatiously at you. With moist sticky hands, he pats your cheek. And suddenly you can't bear it, that some day, all too soon, this one too will be skipping down the walk, and there won't be anybody else to hold up to the window.

"Wait, take it easy, won't you?" you plead foolishly, even as you put him down to start the dishes. "Don't hurry!"

♥ ♥ ♥

MY FAVORITE NEIGHBOR SAYS

After a harried day of settling squabbles
in the yard and getting older kids off to camp
—"I feel like a tossed salad."

28

THE PLAYGROUND

You stroll one night with a very small daughter onto the school playground.

She is enchanted with its wonders. Cleared of all the threat and noisy appropriation of those giants, school children, it is like a toy shop after hours, a circus free for roving—hers alone.

"C'mon, Mommy, push me, watch me ride the merry-go-round." She clambers onto the silvery arc, tilted slightly under a sky that is softly layered with clouds. Her feet jut. She clutches the bars, laughing joyfully as you give it a spin, more and more excited as you sometimes run beside it to increase its speed.

"Faster, faster!" she pleads, hair flying, eyes ecstatic. "You ride too!" And breathless you climb on and watch the world go round.

At length she slides off and scampers over to the jungle gym. "Watch this trick, see me!" Hooking bare knees over a bar she dangles, albeit still clutching tight with her hands.

Her hair swings almost to the ground; her upside-down face is a happy blur in the gathering dusk. The sky clears its throat with a gentle thunder, though here and there it wears a star.

"Watch how high I can go." Cautiously she reaches up, swings on her tummy a minute, maneuvers right and left, and finally drops to the ground. "Now let's go ride the see-saws."

You circle the big motherly looking building that seems to be resting after a hard day. The see-saws stand patiently aslant, awaiting one more pair of straddling legs. The small rider mounts, grasps a handle, bounces futilely, bumping against the ground. At the opposite end you reach high, pull the board against the slight weight it holds. Up and down making up rhymes about the horses you always pretend they are:

> This is a horse whose name is Joe
> Oh, how fast this horse will go!
> This is a horse whose name is Roy,
> Riding him is such a joy.
> This is a horse whose name is Pete—
> He goes swiftly down the street!

Her little skirt puffs as she rides the imaginary steed against the darkening sky. Moving nearer to her end, you sit on the oblique board yourself and ride the see-saw together, striking a balance.

The thunder decides to grumble now. Lightning competes with the stars. A few frail drops touch your cheeks. "C'mon, honey," you say, "this horse is tired, we'd better hit the trail." Lifting her from the see-saw, you hoist her to your back and gallop home.

♥ ♥ ♥

THE SMALL FRY SAY

> Three little folks playing with a coaster wagon. . . First little guy: "Put her in it."
> Second little guy: "Her ain't a her, she's a him."
> First little guy: "I know she is."

30

MATERNAL MAGIC

You sit at the table, reading the paper and having your coffee in those few blessed moments stolen before you must get up and clear the dishes—a part of you tuned, like a radio set turned low, to the children playing outside.

Suddenly the volume rises, there is a yell, somebody is crying, hard. Somebody's hurt! you realize. And for an instant your whole being leaps in instinctive response.

Then in the next flash you are analyzing it, listening for the particular tone of sob or howl that will identify it as your child's. If not, whose? And just what is the degree of anguish? Nature itself seems to warn you when you should dash to the door to offer aid. Or when it is safe to take another sip and turn the page.

If the front door slams, and the voices and crying draw nearer, you know that whoever it is is being brought to you. Even then a mother becomes equipped with a little gauge that enables her to put off this minor trouble, this interruption, this latest demand upon her time, her strength. It will reach her fast enough, she has learned.

"We were playing Red Light and Mary fell down and skinned her leg," sympathetic friends present the bowed and weeping one.

"Oh, what a shame," you cluck, examining it. Carrying your coffee cup in one hand, leading a child by the other, you make for the medicine cabinet.

Nothing serious, thank goodness. Nothing that can't be fixed with a little motherly magic. "First we'll kiss it to make it well, then which do you choose—a pink or a yellow bandaid?"

♥ ♥ ♥

THAT'S WHAT MOTHERS ARE FOR

"That's what mothers are for," she said
When thanked for combing a tumbled head,
Or spreading a slice of jelly-bread—
"That's what mothers are for."

"That's what mothers are for," she smiled,
Soothing the sobs of a frightened child,
Ironing a dress from a basket piled—
"That's what mothers are for."

"That's what mothers are for—" Today
When my own children rush in from play
To be mended or cuddled or helped on their way
Her voice echoes as I too say:
"That's what mothers are for!"

FOUR-LEAF CLOVER

Few of us outgrow the thrill of finding a four-leaf clover.

Hanging out clothes one day you drop a clothespin—and retrieving it behold—the magical combination! With a cry of delight, you summon a child. "How would you like to find a four-leaf clover?"

"Really, could I? And then have good luck all day?"

"Yes, I'm sure there must be at least one here, maybe more."

Excitedly, she hails a playmate. You see them squatting among the fragrant grasses, crawling about on hands and knees. The sunlight spills on their braids, and their faded blue jeans. Their faces are eager. A shout goes up, and one of them rushes to you.

"Is this one?"

"No, honey," you regret to explain, "That's only a different bigger clover, with its third leaf torn."

Back to the hunt, undiscouraged. For there is no faith like that of a child. It will be there, it must. Lurking among the blossoms and the humbler three leaves—the touchstone to certain good fortune and joy. And sure enough, "I found one, I found one!" And almost immediately, "Me too, I did too!"

"Mine's bigger.". . . "That doesn't matter, they're both good luck. See—" Awed, they present their tiny prizes in cupped fingers. And you marvel over them and promise to keep them safe in a dish while they hunt for more. And they find them, well nigh a whole patch, and go into ecstasies about how their luck is sure to last for weeks, months, years. And how they must guard the secret source.

"We don't want Jimmy and his gang raiding our lucky patch.". . .

How swiftly greed sets in; you think—and the anxieties of possession. Then they go commercial. Begin to reason: "Hey, maybe we could tell some kids, just a few, for a penny or maybe a nickel?"

"Yes, but suppose they went and told somebody *else?*"

"Oh, don't worry, just enjoy what you have," you interrupt the haggling. "And share it. Let everybody else be lucky too."

"That's right. After all we found the patch so we've *got* to be lucky. With all that luck it won't *matter* what that Jimmy and his gang might do."

Their faces brighten at this reassurance. And at the prospect of their private share-the-wealth program. "C'mon, let's go tell 'em, we don't have to be mean just because they are. And they might even be nicer to us."

"Hey, that would *really* be good luck!"

"WHO GOES TRIP-TRAP
OVER MY BRIDGE?"

You sit on a little footbridge, the sunlight warm on your bare shoulders, the planks rough and hot to the legs. They sway under your little girl's feet as she shouts with childish fierceness, "Who goes trip-trap, trip-trap over my bridge?"

She sits down then and peels off her sandals. "C'mon, Mommy, let's wade."

The water is icy to the ankles, and the color of an amber, tingling wine. It trails its silver ripples about the pink-gray rocks that rise above it, warm and dry in the sun. Minnows dart about the mossy stones at the bottom, in shadowy schools, elusive as thoughts.

"Where do minnows go so fast? Why're they in such a hurry?"

Yes, why? you too wonder. People aren't the only ones who dash about witlessly. But there is no witless dashing now, only a lazy progress upstream. Your daughter hops from dry rock to dry rock like a squirrel. She gathers bright stones from the bottom and hurls them, rejoicing in the splash, and proud of the glittering circles made.

"Careful now, don't disturb the cows."

For you are approaching their leafy haven. You climb upon a swaying pole fence that spans the creek and peer into a shady, tree-roofed room. Here two copper-colored cows lie chewing, watching you with grave, disinterested eyes. Their hooves have made deep pockets in the mud. And all about them, along

35

the ferny, weeded banks, a whirl of butterflies go dipping in a black-and-gold ballet.

Your youngster sighs. "I just wish they looked a little more mean."

"Why, for goodness sake?"

"Well then it would be more exciting. Kind of like we were the billy goats and here we'd found the real ogres that think they owned the stream."

♥ ♥ ♥

THE SMALL FRY SAY

Accompanied by her small child, the busy mother was shopping in a small town on Saturday night. Recalling at the last minute that she'd forgotten to pick up the pound of butter she'd paid for, she darted back into the store, leaving the child behind on the sidewalk.

Returning to retrieve the youngster, she was asked by her indignant offspring, "What's more important, losing a pound of butter or losing a little girl?"

THE KICKOFF CAN WAIT

C'mon, Mother, let's go exploring. Let's take a hike like you promised we might today, and see what interesting things we can find for school."

Oh, dear, you think, for the football game's about to begin. "Well, just a little one," you tell her. "Let's make it a ten-minute hike, huh?" Though you feel a bit guilty—for how many interesting objects can you possibly find in such a hurry?

Still, you set off up the hillside, where the ground has a crackling softness underfoot, and the sun pours down in a paisley pattern through the burnished leaves.

You tour a little by-path, hunting, hastily hunting, unworthily conscious of the spirited college music that is rising from the porch, the awareness of players trotting onfield.

But there, in a crush of brittle bended grasses is a bird's nest, which you both spy with a shout. And she scoops up its frail weavings and tucks it into her shoebox treasure chest.

"And moss, look at the lovely green moss!" she exclaims.

And you do look, with eyes that are quickly aware, and find a starry pattern in its thick velvet cushion. Into the box that too.

And now you find, on the rocky hillside, a bright outcropping that sparkles in the sun. "Ah, my turn now—there's a geode," you inform her. "I remember those from geology class. See— a geode; that's a rock that some bright crystals have grown on."

"A geode," she repeats in wonder, holding it up. "Why, it's like a precious jewel."

And just across the road are leaves of some rare and exquisite shape, and spiky lavender flowers. And behind them a bending branch strung with a fringe of dusty gray-purple fronds that you surely must have. And then, bowing like parasoled ladies at a party, a tall clutch of blooms.

"Look, look, parasols!" Your small companion points excitedly.

They rise across a drift of drying growths, but whether fruit or flower you cannot say. Only that a hard little scarlet shell has broken into five arching fingers, from which dance delicate pendants of purple and gold. What they are you do not know, simply that you must have them too, no matter who wins the toss at the football game.

"Better hurry. You've missed the kickoff," your husband shouts.

"Who cares?" You wink at your child.

"That's right." She screws up her face to wink back. "Wait'll he sees our treasures, he'll be sorry he didn't come along!"

CURIOSITY BUNDLE

Steak's about ready, everybody hurry up!" your husband calls, presiding over the barbecue. "Mmmm, smells divine. Like incense in a temple," you exclaim as the red coals pop and sizzle, and aromatic blue smoke drifts upward in the light of late afternoon.

"What's divine?" a small voice demands. "What's incense in a temple?"

Preoccupied with counting out paper plates, you don't reply. "Tell me things," the little one persists, clambering onto the long pine table and sitting thoughtful, chin in hand. "Tell me lots of things I don't know yet."

"Now? Oh, honey, not just yet. Get down." For the clan is gathering. Like a school of fish before the bait they come scurrying, leaping from boats, shedding towels from swimming, stubbing toes and howling, slamming doors.

The charred brown succulence is forked grandly onto an enormous platter, borne in state toward the table on the porch, and portioned out. "He got the biggest piece!". . . "Mine's dirty!". . . "Honey, that's just the charcoal, it won't hurt you—adds flavor. Dear, this is really ambrosia—"

"What's ambrosia?" pipes up the persistent seeker after knowledge. "Where does charcoal come from? Why do people like to eat outdoors?"

The last, at least, you can answer. "Because things taste better." You draw a deep appreciative breath. "When the air's so fresh and you can smell the water and see the sunset and hear the birds getting ready for bed—"

"How do birds get ready for bed? Do they have to take off their feathers and put on pajamas?"

This prospect is so delightful that even she shouts with laughter and plunges into your lap.

The others have finished already. They have wolfed down the meat like hungry cubs and rushed back to their activities, trying to cram in as much as possible before dark. Your husband has strolled back to the barbecue. There is a hissing, a puff of white smoke as he thriftily douses the coals to be used another time.

"Now let's see, what were some of the things you wanted to know about? Incense, for one. And charcoal—" You are alone at the cluttered table holding a small warm bundle of curiosity on your lap.

THE ARTIST IN EVERY CHILD

A child's feeling for art is a strange and wonderful thing.

He clutches a crayon or pencil and tries to make it speak for him, often before he can otherwise express himself at all. His first efforts are wild and wonderful attacks upon the nearest surface, whether it be paper, picture book, or the family walls.

With vigor and joy he makes these glorious swatches of color, and no matter if they adhere to the firm outlines of the puppy, the flower, or the little girl in the fat soft book that has been provided for him.

With equal vigor and delight he loves to draw. His first efforts at depicting a man are marvels of simplicity—a round shape, usually, with a few sticks of sprouting limbs. Gradually, as his powers of observation and duplication come into focus, he adds the facial features and the refinements of clothes.

Animals likewise grow under his fingers, fierce or gentle, according to his mood; and the sun in the sky burns a hot yellow, jutting rays like porcupine quills.

A child is truly an artist, no matter how lopsided or out of proportion his efforts, for in this early stage of his being he shares the emotions that the genuine artist knows: The sheer joy of creating, which hurls him bodily into his work. The child feels the hot sunlight he has beating down upon the cottage roof, runs in terror along with his Goldilocks, knows the forlorn disappointment of his three well-meaning bears.

This is the essence of a youngster's art. His

capacity to live fully in the act of depicting. He bolts into a vivid world of color and action, of jagged seas and tossing ships, where he can stand on the bridge in command, or swim with the fishes beneath the brilliant blue waves.

And this selfsame quality of participation he brings to the pictures he sees. The comic strips are a world in microcosm, each frame a little stage. Without bothersome mental gymnastics, he is swept into the activities of their boldly drawn characters, who seem so real, not because of what they say but because of the way they are shown.

And their backgrounds! I still remember vividly the furnishings in Jiggs' and Maggie's house (those Oriental vases!) and Maggie's hair styles, and shrew though she was—her dashing wardrobes.

Children's illustrators know well this innate need of childhood to be captured by that rectangle into which the artist must compress all the magic at his fingertips. To be successful it must engage the child's emotions, his senses, so that he will pore over the scene and scarcely be able to leave it. Mrs. Dagmar Wilson, who has done so many children's books, says, "The nicest compliment I can hear is for a child to say, 'I'd like to be in that picture.' For you know when he says that, in his imagination he's already there."

♥ ♥ ♥

OFFSPRING ART

"What are you going to call your painting, Jan?"
"Right now I call it quits!"

42

SAFE HARBOR

If only you could lead children safely through life, you think, the way you can lead them across a busy street.

A busy thoroughfare goes past our house, and beyond that flashing river of cars lies the daily objective, the school playground. "Take us across, Mother," they ask, day after day. "And when we're through playing we'll yell for you to come bring us home."

And so you take them and sometimes a whole chain of playmates by the hand, and usher them to safe harbor. And when they've finished playing, they stand on the curb and call until you hear them and make the trip again to lead them home.

If only you could lead them as safely and surely through life! But you know—for you've watched the others grow older, that time teaches them to look after themselves. To wait, to look carefully in all directions, and then when their own intelligence directs, to march courageously on to their destinations.

When that time comes they won't be asking you to hold their hands—only saying, "Let me go!" And you can't help very much when they get to the other side. No matter what happens, there won't be any curbs to stand on calling, "Mother!" Or if there are, they'll be too proud to use them and you'll be too far away to hear.

Life has to be like that. And it's what we really

want. Not for the voice calling, "Mother, come get me, I want to come home!" But stating confidently, "I'm here, safely here, and I made it on my own."

♥ ♥ ♥

MEMORY PICTURES

A little boy wriggling importantly on his back beneath his pedal car, and hammering vigorously away in the manner of his dad...

The enchanted expression on a toddler's face as you summon her to the phone, and the shy giggling wonder with which she listens, too impressed even to reply...

School children boarding an excursion bus, their bright faces beaming out the windows, waving to fond mothers watching from porches as they pass...

Two pajama-clad sons playing horse at bedtime, the older snorting and cavorting and bucking about on all fours, while the younger rides him with a beaming, almost placid glee...

Singing the old lullaby, "Baby's Boat's a Silver Moon," as you rock the youngest to sleep one night—and later, when you go to the crib, finding, as if by magic, a tiny silver canoe of a moon anchored in the window overhead.

WHEN CAN HE GO FISHING?

They are dipping for minnows at the corner where the creek bends, for they are going fishing in the morning.

It is dusk, drawing dark, and as you attend to last minute tasks in the breakfast room the light illuminates the entire back yard. It is as if clean silver pencils have lightly sketched the outlines of the trees and underscored the leaves in gently dancing lines.

You fold away the last of the ironing and go out to be with them. You cross the damp, cool grass and call out to the toddler who is earnestly clambering up and down the rock steps on little errands they have thought up for him, for he wants to help.

"Fish, my fish!" he proudly exhibits three frantic minnows darting about in his little sand bucket. "I caught some too."

You cuddle him onto your lap there on the topmost step. There is the scent of leaf mold and fern and tangy growing things. The water below you is black liquid silver, scolding and chortling as it tumbles over the rock dam your husband and sons have built.

The far light from the kitchen window traces the outlines of their heads and their earnest faces bending to seek out the secret darting life in the water at their feet. One son is sensibly wearing boots to protect his feet. Their buckles rattle as he sloshes about and the rubber gleams. The other is barefoot, nimble as a sprite.

Your husband, pant-legs rolled up, waves at you and proceeds with the business at hand. The net is lifted and flipping bodies pour into the bucket in a bright cascade.

"Man, they're really asking to be caught tonight!"

"When will I be old enough to go fishing too?" the little one forlornly asks.

"Too soon," you inform him, carrying him and his little pail back toward the kitchen light. "Don't hurry!"

HAVE YOU EVER WONDERED WHY

Childhood diseases so seldom strike your crop of candidates all at once, but trail out chain-reaction fashion so as to keep you confined to the house for weeks. . .

When you take them to the movies they always have to be hastened to the bathroom in the middle of a big love scene?

CHILDREN'S BUILT-IN METRONOMES

Children have a natural affinity for rhythms and poems and songs.

The baby in his crib croons and sings to himself in a tempo that could almost be measured with a metronome. The toddler trots away rhythmically on his stubby shoes. He learns to march early and takes vast delight in it. Still drooling, he will adorn himself in a too-small bonnet or a father's big hat, and banging on a lid, strut around to music, keeping time.

He tries to dance early. It is almost instinctive for very young children to begin to bounce and wave their hands and prance about when they hear songs.

"See, he's going to be a dancer," parents proudly point out. And the curve of a young child's fingers is indeed like a ballerina's, relaxed and supple, like the petals of a flower.

Even when a child falls, he does so with a kind of liquid collapsing, as if he is in mysterious harmony with the tides and pulses of the universe. Perhaps this is why he seldom hurts himself seriously or breaks bones.

Children love rhymes and chants; it doesn't matter so much what they say as the jingle and beat of how. As soon as they can talk, children make up rhymes and chants of their own. Every mother who listens can hear gems like this as a youngster swings or plays in the sandpile or sits building blocks or merely trots around:

"Oh-oh-oh, me-me, I am so happy. Oh-oh-oh, my, what makes the sky, and what makes the birdies toooo? Oh-oh-oh, my—!"

Sometimes the ideas and combinations are lovely, sometimes funny, but invariably they are bits of pure uninhibited free-wheeling poetry.

Later when a child has mastered language, he loves to write verses down. He is fascinated by the very limitations of metre now, the wonderful puzzle of finding words that rhyme.

Again the results may be comical and awkward, but often delicate and lovely and wonderful in their concepts. The medium is like a harness into which he strives to fit his rhythmic spirit, and though the harness is strange and jangling, yet the joy he feels in it is strong.

And children love to read poems and have them read to them. Each year at the bookstall at our school fair they come asking for "poem books." And sad to say, there are not many to offer them. Thousands of books of other types are published, but not many people write poems for children any more. Where is today's Eugene Field or James Whitcomb Riley?

For that matter, where are the lyric poets who used to speak the language of the people for all the rest of us? The Sara Teasdales and Edna St. Vincent Millays? The Joyce Kilmers and Lew Saretts and Robert Frosts?

In any case, children are nature's own poets . . . part and parcel of the essential singing stanzas of life.

"LET'S EAT ON THE WAY"

You look tired, honey," your husband says as you fly along the highway to your country cabin one weekend. "Would you like to stop and eat somewhere?"

He's right, you are bone-weary, and the thought of cooking looms as a burden. "Well, if we could find someplace quick. Say a drive-in where we could have a cup of coffee and then go on—."

"Good idea, there's a nice one not too far ahead." And soon you see its beckoning, gaily colored tubes of light, and swing out of the swift Friday night traffic that flings a blazing ruby chain the length of the highway.

"Oh boy, oh boy!" the youngsters begin to shout their enthusiastic approval. (What is it about merely stopping for food that signals such mad delight?)

Orders begin to fly: Cheeseburgers, barbecues with lots of onion and mustard, French fries, hot dogs, double-thick milk shakes. "Can I get out? Can I go too and help carry?" they beg.

Surrounded and trailed by offspring, your husband trudges up to the counter of the pagoda-shaped glass house that is so white and shining it might be an operating room.

The dog, sensing food, braces big paws on the back-seat and barks a futile order too. The cat, heavy with her own potential family, prowls the dashboard and whines.

You've learned from sad experience it's better

not to feed them before leaving home.

Oh dear, how will you ever manage when the family returns with all that food?

Here they come now, gingerly clutching their paper cups and bags. "Here y'are, Mom, we got you a hamburger and milkshake along with the coffee. Pep you up."

You accept the hot, oniony smelling package, and begin to maneuver the hot and the cold paper cups. The baby wakes and begins to fret; the dog and cat are frantic; people climb all over your legs, your lap. But somehow you get a sip of the coffee, a gulp of the milkshake, a bite of the bun. "Mmmm, delicious.

"Oh, be careful, let's not spill. Hush, darling, where's your bottle? Down, Belle, down, give her a bite somebody. Somebody catch the cat! Oh dear, they're starved, give the kitty a few French fries, they won't hurt her. Be patient, your supper's coming—"

"Well, everybody ready?" Munching, your husband steps on the starter. Thank goodness he's so expert at the wheel. You inch over to give him more room. The coffee is reviving. The sandwich warm and thick. The chocolate milkshake rich—in the snatched moments when you can get to them.

But it's worth the struggle. The radio is playing a lively tune. The children are too occupied with eating to argue... And you won't have to cook when you arrive!

YOU MAY LEAD A CHILD TO CULTURE
BUT . . .

A young woman expecting her first baby once wrote to tell me how she was going to stimulate a love of the arts in her young.

"We had few books in my home, so I'm going to surround him with them. Fortunately, art galleries are free, so we're going to take him to see the great pictures (I've already begun cutting reproductions from the magazines).

"And I think if a child hears good music from the beginning, he won't want any other kind. We're going to have lots of fine records, and take him to symphonies even if he doesn't have shoes!"

All that is commendable—but it made me think of Arturo (named for Toscanini, his mother's favorite conductor). Arty was raised on a college campus— and if ever a child was dipped in the font of culture he was it. One of his pre-school parlor tricks was to go through a big book of Famous Paintings, identifying each one.

He could hum the arias from operas and tell you their stories. No Three Bears and Little Red Hens for him—he was on cozier terms with Sir Gawain and Gulliver and Oedipus Rex.

But by the time Arturo was in his teens, he couldn't be dragged to a concert, or cajoled into reading even the campus newspaper.

When he got up his own little band it wasn't Beethoven they played. Having flunked out of college,

51

he married the girl singer and very happily took up farming, where he's ardent only about the culture of corn and pigs!

All of which seems to prove that there's actually danger of over-exposure. Drag a child to concerts too often too young, and he's liable to develop a life-long antipathy for music he neither enjoyed nor understood.

Haul youngsters to art galleries, and brace yourself—instead of gazing with the desired awe at Titians or Rembrandts, they're likely to start chasing each other along the corridors.

Read to them, by all means. Buy and borrow books. But be forewarned. However diligent your efforts, unless they have a natural love of reading, many will not be caught dead reading a book later on.

I'm afraid love of the arts is innate; it comes with the individual child. It is a need of his inmost nature, and will grow of itself. I don't think you can hurt it very much by neglect, nor foster it very much through attention. Certainly you can't graft it on from outside.

Kids are contrary creatures. The values parents most desperately want for them, are often the very values they spurn. Often it takes a stranger—an admired teacher, friend or sweetheart to inspire them toward wanting the "better things" that parents have been hopefully offering all the time.

Meanwhile, example is more effective than exhortation. About all you can do is go on enjoying these things yourself; and if the child would seek entrance to your lovely garden, make him welcome. But he can't be dragged or driven or, however lovingly, transplanted there against his will.

Curiously, some of our greatest artistic geniuses had parents who didn't know a classic from a comic strip.

♥ ♥ ♥

WHIMSICAL SIGHTS OF SUMMER

Two little kids in business behind a cardboard box and a pitcher, with a sign which says: "Lemonade 2¢ half a glass, 5¢ whole glass."

♥ ♥ ♥

THE SMALL FRY SAY

"When Daddy gives me a good talking to it hurts me worse than a spanking would. You may think I'm just saying that to get out of spankings, but I'm not." Thoughtfully—"You haven't had a spanking in years, have you?" . . .

Three-year-old: "I don't take naps, I'm not the type." . . . *After a rain: "Oh, look, look, the flowers have a wading pool!"* . . . *"If I just had to have one of my eyes knocked out, I'd rather it would be this one, because I can wink the other one."* . . .

After glancing around the table and discovering broccoli: "Dear Lord, for practically all the food we are about to receive we offer our thanks."

THE WONDER OF WATCHING A TRAIN

No matter how sophisticated we become in this jet age, most of us will never outgrow the thrill and wonder of trains. They are inextricably linked with my midwestern childhood, for we had three depots in our small town to accommodate three lines, and people set their watches by the trains. The most glamorous train was the 8:13 on its way from Sioux City to Chicago. It had a dining car and sleepers, and its passengers gazing down were like gods and goddesses on Olympus. To meet somebody or see somebody off on the 8:13— what a thrill. And to think of some day actually *taking* it—!

The freight trains lumbered constantly through town, hauling grain and livestock to market. The engines burned wood and coal, giant ladies who hurled their magnificent manes of curly hair, black or white, against the blue skies. Their bells clanged imperiously, their whistles shrilled and sang.

We often awoke to hear the trains switching in the night, shuffling forward, wrenching backward with a great clatter, burdened, driven, mysterious those great labored feet in the darkness. The engines would shudder, as if in a huge paroxysm of emotion; then after a series of little sighs and squalls and squeals and clankings, they finally struggled off, chuffing faster and faster, gathering breath and speed until finally the rhythms ran free. . . free. . . . So that you wanted to rise from your bed and run to catch up, climb aboard, soar away with it—that glorious force delivered of its burden of boxcars or coalcars or freight.

A hoot, a distant plaintive cry of farewell, and gradually the rhythms faded, were lost, and once again the night was still. . .

Trains will always be favorite toys for children (and their fathers) and they love to watch "choo-choo trains." When mine were small we lived in a city only a few blocks from a railroad track. It became a daily ritual to load up the baby and a couple of toddlers, ours and sometimes neighbors' and push through the morning to await the 11:05. Enroute, we would dip into a small fragrant neighborhood bakery where the proprietor did not disdain to sell us three or four big sugar cookies, 2¢ each.

The treats were portioned out, to be nibbled in eager bliss awaiting the arrival of the train. "When's it coming, Mommy? Where's the choo-choo train?"

"It's coming, it'll be here any minute. Listen, can you hear it?"

Heads cocked, eyes widened, everyone strained to be first to spy it and announce: *"Train, train,* choo-choo train!" Emitting its cry of joy and welcome it would round the bend, come pounding toward you, this great black dragon of delight, while the children shrank back in an ecstasy of fear even as they waved.

And the engineer and the fireman would smile down and lift gloved hands in the eternal salute to children. And even the baby, cowering in your arms, would lift an awed face and uncoil a tiny fist, like an opening flower, in return. And as the cars glided by, filled with passengers gazing down, some of them too always waved.

May trains never vanish; may more and more of them come back. There is nothing quite like the thrill and wonder of a train.

WOULDN'T YOU LIKE A DIME EVERY TIME?

You've ducked a snowball?... Thrown one back... Pulled small fry on sleds... Brushed them off when they fell down... Made them wipe their feet... Comforted a nose-runny, weepy one with stinging fingers who's played outside too long?

♥ ♥ ♥

I SPANKED MY CHILD TODAY

I spanked my child today.
She'd torn her dress at play,
And tracked across the rug,
And laughed at me with such a smug
Defiant, impish way
I sort of lost my head.
I spanked her till her little
Spanking place was red . . .
But now that she's in bed
I don't know what to say . . .
A sleeping child is such a tender sight.
One hand upflung against the pillow white.
A toy still clutched; the fair hair mussed . . .
If I've betrayed Your sacred trust,
Oh, Lord of little children, please forgive,
And let me live
Tomorrow to outweigh.
I wish I hadn't spanked my child today.

CHILDREN AND SOLITUDE

Reading A.A. Milne's poem "Solitude" (from *Now We Are Six*) the little one asks, "What's solitude?"

"Solitude," you remark wryly, "is something a mother seldom has." And then you hasten to explain, "Solitude is being alone."

She regards you, puzzled. "Is it nice to be alone?"

"Sometimes it's very nice indeed. If you're not lonely, that is. Loneliness is a sad kind of being alone. Solitude is—well, peaceful, quiet; a chance to be yourself, to think your own thoughts and do things you don't have time for with people around. At least that's how it seems to me."

"I know." She emits an immense sigh. "Sometimes I like to be all by myself, to go play dolls or just sit and watch a bug in the grass."

And you think—why yes, that's true. Children, closer actually to many of the fundamentals which nourish growth, have a strange instinct for solitude.

Yes, they must have playmates. A healthy horde of noisy, fighting, friendly companions. And clubs, either of their own spontaneous devising, or Brownies, Bluebirds, Cubs and all the other earnest herdings with which we adults foster group spirit and often make it difficult for them or ourselves to enjoy any genuine solitude.

But children recognize this need even if they don't know its name. And they have their own ways of getting it. I wonder if some of those days when they play sick to keep from going to school aren't actually a kind of ruse to lie abed with books and dolls and favorite toys and enjoy a little pure solitude?

Older youngsters are often quite clear and adamant about their desire for solitude. "Leave me alone!" they demand, and the phrase means exactly that. Or they will bolt their bedroom doors and tack blatant warnings on them: "Keep out. This means YOU!"

And nothing does more for their egos, and perhaps for their self-reliance, than to be allowed to keep a household going while the rest of the family are away.

"I don't need anybody to come look after me, for Pete's sake, and I don't want to go stay with Bill. I'll be okay, honest— I *want* to stay alone!"

And you invest in a week's supply of TV dinners, leave a key and many instructions, alert the neighbors, and take off. And on your return are greeted by a house no more messy than you expected, and a grinning, proud and thoroughly satisfied son.

"Gee, there was nothing to it. In fact it was swell. With nobody yakking at me, I got all my homework caught up and read and worked on my fishing tackle and got to bed early every night, no kidding. Boy, it was wonderful—gimme more of this thing you call *solitude!*"

CLEVER HIDING PLACES

What is this curious, comical, exasperating, yet somehow charming instinct children have for hiding? Either possessions or themselves.

Often the major appeal of a house or yard is its hiding places. An attic with crannies and cubbies, a garage with a "secret" loft, an immense old shielding tree. To steal away, to scurry out of sight, to crouch hidden and breathless, heart pounding, trying to outwit or outwait the search party, whether anxious parents, or playmates in a game. As even adults can remember—what excruciating fun.

And small children have a squirrel-like penchant for hiding things—toys, candy or even their own clothing. Two of ours once hid under the bed, and while there the little boy stuffed his shoes up between the mattress and the spring. Later when the shoes turned up missing, both children cheerfully joined in the frantic hunt. And his sister was positively beaming when at last she decided to lead the family to the clever hiding place.

Once my cousin had made a beautiful dress in home economics which she brought home for her mother to press. When she wasn't looking, a small nephew was inspired to steal off with it. When the dress could not be found, sheer bedlam ensued. The entire family spent most of the night combing the house; yet that dress, which was due for an exhibit the next day, was simply nowhere to be found. In desperation her mother arose at dawn and whipped up a duplicate, so my cousin could be in the display.

Months passed, with absolutely no clue to the mystery of the vanished dress. Until, opening the big dining table wider one day for company, there, incredibly was the dress! That little guy had, for reasons unknown, wadded it up and stuffed it out of sight in the space beneath the leaves.

♥ ♥ ♥

MOTHER, DON'T STEAL THE SHOW!

A letter from a young mother who used to be a professional dancer and teacher reflects a common contradiction: "Occasionally I practice a bit on neighborhood children. I'm a big hit with the handspring and walkovers and splits—nobody else's mother can do them. But curiously, or maybe not so curiously, my little girls are embarrassed when I show off. And looking back, I guess I don't blame them—I remember how I used to be embarrassed at my own mother's agile tricks. Aren't children incomprehensible? The truth is, they don't want to watch you—they only want you watching and marveling over them."

SWING INTO OUTER SPACE

C'mon, Mommy, swing me!" the little one pleads. Let's play sun, moon and stars."

You put her off as long as you can, but finally, conscience nagging, take her hand and head for the swing in the yard. Lifting her in, you begin to push, reciting the chant that, in a mad moment's invention, accompanies this game.

"All abooard! Tickets ready? Space ship departing for Mars, Jupiter, Venus and all planets west."

"No, Mother, that's not right," you are corrected, for a child's memory puts an elephant's to shame, "first we go to the sun and the moon and *then* the stars."

"Okay," you laugh, though an astronomer would have a few protests of his own. "Tickets, tickets."

She produces a crumpled leaf. Wriggling around, "And don't forget the scary part taking off."

"Scary part?"

"Oh, Mommy, you remember! It's where I almost fall out."

"All right, fasten your seat belts, folks, these jet engines make it pretty dangerous."

She squeals delightedly as you yank the swing from side to side, jerk it, pretend to try and shake her out. Then she is skimming up and up and you are going through the rigamarole (oh, foolish day) you long ago began. About the blinding light of the sun, the pearly glow of the moon, about the wealth of jewels to be found and gathered up at each starry stop.

"I know what," she cries when you complain that you are tired and try various ruses to call the whole thing off—"*you* be the passenger!"

So you flop obediently into the swing; you suffer yourself to be jerked and twisted about. Puffing with the effort, she nudges you forward a few inches and back. "See, I can do it, I'm pushing you!"

"You certainly are," you say, subtly beginning to pump. Higher and higher you go, till your feet brush leaves. The sky dips close; the sun's gold flames. A queer excitement grips you. The treasures are there, they truly are! You glimpse them, you almost touch them—through a child's make-believe.

THE WORLD'S MOST LOVING
LISTENERS

How much of a parent's life is spent on chants and drills. On ABC's and spelling lists and multiplication tables. On giving cues for plays, or patiently teaching that classic, The Gettysburg Address. How often a book is propped as the dishes are washed or potatoes peeled. *"Indefinite,"* you pronounce.

"Indefinite," the child repeats, "I-n-d-e-f-e-n-"

"No, dear," you correct. "It's an I after the F. Listen to how it sounds."

Or the ancient singsong of the tables: "Eight times four is thirty-two. Eight times five is FOR-ty. . ."

Or, wiping your hands, you find your place in the script for the junior play. "Okay, now I'll be Mr. Bowers. 'How *dare* you wake me up at this hour of the night?' " You look up, urge, "Come on, come on, that's your cue—you're Sam."

"Aaah, Mom, I know, but do you have to be so darned dramatic?"

"All right, I'll try to read it straight." Deadpan, "There was a break-in at the plant."

Son (or Sam) self-consciously: "Then call the police, this means trouble."

"Oh, come on now, darling, you can do better than that. Get some emotion into your voice."

"Look, this isn't dress rehearsal or anything. I just wanta learn my part!"

Or, regularly as robins or crocuses or Lincoln's birthday, the immortal words: "Fourscore and seven years ago, our fathers brought forth on this continent a new nation, conceived in liberty and dedicated to the proposition—"

(That mothers should be audience to these phrases forever. It occurs to you—good heavens, maybe these lines wouldn't have endured so long if it hadn't been for us). . .

Or, "The quality of mercy is not strained; it droppeth as the gentle rain from heaven upon the place beneath—"

(The place beneath. . . A kitchen stove. A dining table. A bedroom, the laundry tubs. Wherever can be found those longsuffering listeners, mothers.)

"It is twice blest. It blesseth"— him that pours, you realize, and her that receives.

For they draw you close, these sessions, with the child striving to master the words so familiar you could chant them in your sleep. (Don't rush him, don't show your weariness, remember the parent who listened so patiently to you.) They become a kind of communion.

"Thanks, Mom, I think I've got it now."

"All right if you're sure—but if you want to take it one more time—"

THE PERFECT GIFT—A DAY ALONE

One of the nicest presents any busy mother could have would be, I think, a day all to herself. On Mother's Day, yes, she wants to be surrounded by her clan. But later the gift of a day—even a few hours' solitude, would be bliss.

To find the house suddenly, completely cleared. To hear no voices, banging doors, or running feet. To be pestered by no chores. To be free to think— I'm me! Nobody needs or wants me. Within this golden frame of time I can do exactly what I wish.

It's a little bit like being a child released in a dime store, with a dazzling but limited amount to spend. Oh, so many fascinating things from which to choose. Let's see, what are some of the enticing things continually put off because you can't enjoy them with interruptions?

First, shall you make fresh coffee and really luxuriate over the paper? Or tackle that reproachful heap of unread magazines? Or the books you've been longing to read? No, the books defeat you from the start. All beg so lustily for attention, and if you settle down to one you'll be hooked. This whole precious day will be gone.

How about a baking spree? It's impossible to do justice to luscious sounding recipes with children climbing on stools to watch, or clamoring for turns. . . Oh, but what a pity to spend this golden time in a kitchen where you're already forced to do duty thrice a day.

The garden, then, the flowers? To be able to transplant, weed, or just dream in the dirt on your knees without having to stop, or have little folks underfoot—how divine.

Or write in your journal? Answer letters? Paint a picture? Work on a scrapbook? Sort beads and buttons and dress materials? Make a hat? . . .

Oh, the lovely, tantalizing possibilities of filling a day, or even a few solitary hours. If you really want to give Mother a gift she'll treasure and remember—present her with a shining package of time.

MOTHER, COWARDLY LION

C'mon," they invite. "Come to the lake
with us and we'll show you our camping place and a
path to an old abandoned house."

You eye them—the small girl, the boy, the dog,
Spooky, and their Eskimo friend, Terrence, whose
slanty eyes twinkle and whose hair is as crisply black
as Spooky's flanks.

"We show you how to shoot turtles." He
grins—the words less an accent than a singing nasal
twang.

"Okay," you say, and follow the dog, who scrambles, after some hesitation, into the boat.

The lake is a steely-glass sheet that mirrors the
trees to perfection, and every bright small boat. Leaning over you see the vast curved upside-down world in
which the sky becomes a pavement cobbled with
clouds.

But the children watch only the turtles sunning
themselves on upjutting logs. Skinny necks and heads
protruding, they layer each other three deep, like
bowls. "Man, lookit 'em!" The middle boy cuts the
motor; both young hunters raise their trusty BB guns.

Sput... sput... sput. The ineffective shots
glance harmlessly right and left of the game, bounce
beady on the water, or occasionally tick off a shell.
The turtles skid hastily into the water, flipping over to
show their bellies, yellow in the sun.

"Think I could hit a heron?"

"Don't you try," you warn—and all turn to

watch it stalking in the shallows, tall, ugly-graceful as it moves on stilted legs. "Oh, there it goes!" With a great swoop and flap of wings it rises, emitting its odd creaking cry.

You tie up at a clearing and are shown the place where they made camp the day before.

"Now we'll take you to the abandoned house."

You tramp off through dry sunny grasses to a pathway through the woods. Flowers spurt here and there. A clump of tall bonnet-like blossoms. Frail purple spikes. A flash of scarlet from some rare, lost little bloom. The woods smell rich and spicy—an amalgam of earth, water, leaf mold—like some age-old preservative generated from the body of earth itself, to give savor and permanence to growing things.

Walking the path is somehow like walking the road to the Emerald City, and as you go along you tell Terrence the story of The Wizard of Oz, which he has never heard.

"I'll be Dorothy," says the little girl, "Spooky can be Toto. The boys can be the Woodman and the Scarecrow, and Mother, you be the Cowardly Lion."

"Well, gee, thanks," you laugh, and play the role with gusto—and a kind of wary purpose. You're beginning to feel tired and hot. Also a vague unease. Turtles and campsites are one thing—but you're not too sure about this business of exploring an old abandoned house!

GOING TO CHURCH WITH CHILDREN

One Sunday in church an attractive young mother sat in front of me with two ruffled, beribboned little girls, whose quite natural and harmless squirming was less distracting than the whispered tirade it evoked: "Sit still, I won't have that, don't touch, I'll spank, be quiet, you're bad, won't you ever learn? Mind me, hush, behave!"

Finally, in a burst of exasperation, both were yanked from the pew, one of them fighting sobs of obvious humiliation, the other casting a final wistful glance toward the altar with its cross and baskets of flowers.

And I thought—there is something wrong with this picture of Sunday morning. I visualized the early rising and lengthy effort that must have gone into baths and hair brushings and whitening of shoes, and the finding of gloves and tiny coats. Remembered too the last minute things that can go wrong—purses that can't be found, cars that won't start. Know from experience that Mommy is often tired by the time she gets there. But how sad that the bright moments that should be the climax of all that effort, should end so dismally.

Parents and children are encouraged, rightly, to worship together. But I wonder if there shouldn't be a course in the psychology of their sitting peacefully in a pew?

If so, I wish my Grandpa Griffith were alive to teach it. He was volunteer baby sitter every

Sunday while Mother played the organ. And he herded us all so gently, and so gaily into the back row where he equipped us with pencils and Sunday School papers.

We were free to read the stories, or to draw on the paper's margins. Or he would draw for us himself—I can see them yet, those long-nosed caricatures from his calloused fingers. Or we could curl up against him and drowse. Or he would produce a peppermint, a rabbit's foot or other wonders from his pockets.

All this interspersed with joyous and lively singing of the hymns; behind it the minister's voice, whose words penetrated more deeply than anyone could possibly guess. I still remember some of them vividly.

Outwardly inattentive, our fledgling souls were being forever shaped and etched by that weekly exposure to truth, exhortation and Bible story, in an atmosphere we enjoyed.

Youngsters are at first eager to go to church and Sunday School. Yet how often and how soon they begin to resist, or break away altogether. Can it sometimes be because of parents who dutifully drive them there, then make the whole experience an ordeal?

"Suffer the little children to come unto me and forbid them not," the Lord said. Surely he must have meant to include—"forbid them not the peace and pleasure that should be part of the coming."

THE SENTIMENTAL MOTHER

Are you a sentimental mother? You are if you keep wondering what to do about the following:

Baby shoes—nobody else could possibly use them, and there's a limit even to bronze bookends. But you yearn over the cracks and creases, the stubby wornout toes. . .

Little, thumbed and tattered books—especially those lovingly inscribed by grandparents and doting aunts. Too personal to donate to the school fair, many of them too far gone to keep. And yet—and yet—you see the earnestly bowed heads, hear the laughter at bedtime, and the halting, mispronounced words as a beginning reader struggles to master them.

First papers and drawings and workbooks from school or Sunday School. . . Particularly those with gold stars on them, or a teacher's generously encouraging, "Good!". . .

The lumpy, leaking teddy bear that accompanied the whole family on so many trips. . .

Anniversary and birthday and Mother's Day cards. . .

Old snapshots. Particularly those of your husband when he was a little boy. . .

Those yellowed letters that other members of the family have faithfully saved for years and now present to you with, "Here, take 'em, you can have 'em, they're all yours.". . .

Those cards and notes of congratulation people sent you when the children were born. . .

Each generation of mothers faces this tender problem: How to keep, or dispose of, these battered testimonials to life's experiences.

For the stream of life keeps flowing, and at every turn deposits them at your feet and you can't keep them all, yet you feel such a traitor if you throw them out.

You are, in short, just an old-fashioned sentimental mother.

♥ ♥ ♥

WHIMSICAL WISDOM

"Our guests want to stay up half the night and visit, but they can sleep late the next day. I can't—I've got three little birds waiting on me with their mouths open."

THE FARM

Some midwestern relatives live on the very rim of town.

There is a farm just across the fence, and in the morning you are awakened by the snorting and squealing of pigs, the mooing of cattle, and the rich odor of barns comes up strong in the wind and sun.

"Let's go for a hike," the children say. "Let's go see the farm."

You brave a barbed wire fence, and there it lies before you—the rolling, yellow-green pasture, the long white barns, the board fences and rutted pig yards, all flung against blue sky and fat white clouds, with the lovely touch of white pigeons flying.

Beyond the barn is a shining area of pure brassy gold where oats have just been cut, and behind that the rolling, green-silvery sea of head-high corn.

You choose the stream side of the pasture, at the base of the hill, where clumps of willows stand stately in their pools of shade.

"Oh, look, see the cows!"

They form an unexpected barrier, a sizeable herd of them huddled together, their white faces turned as one to regard your approach.

"Cows won't hurt you," you say reassuringly. "Or—will they?"

They seem so many and so huge, and their concentrated interest is vaguely ominous, particularly when they stamp and begin to move en masse your way. "Hey, let's get out of here!"

"Ah, Mom, c'mon," a boy scoffs bigly, "I walked right past 'em the other day."

"Just the same I don't like their expression."

Your little girl is already dashing ahead of you, to scale a low-slung tree. "Can cows climb trees?"

"No, but I don't want you stranded—you get right down!"

You snatch her from her perch and flee, vaguely ashamed.

The triumphant cows swing their heads to watch your hasty progress up the hill. "I know what, let's go see the pigs."

The pig lots stand tangy and inviting, sharp with nostalgic memories. You climb a shaky board fence and swing to the ground. You peer over another, where the remarkably homely, sharp-nosed pink-eyed pigs are stilting around rooting and snuffing, on their little high heels.

Your son makes snorting noises too, and to his surprise they come trotting up, their pace slowing suspiciously as they draw near.

"Here pig, pig, pig!" The noise startles them; they wheel and bound off, their curly tails comical little question marks.

Your daughter emits an eloquent sigh. "Well—at least we saw one thing scareder of us than we are of it on a farm."

A NIGHT OUT WITH MOM

Now hurry and get your baths, children. Since Dad won't be home till late, I'm taking you to the theatre tonight."

"Oh, boy, a play! But I am clean, I washed my neck real good after baseball practice, I'm okay."

"A neck washing's not enough. When you go to the theatre, you've got to be clean all the way. And I'll lay out your good suit."

"A *suit?*" the agonized wail goes up. "You know that thing itches me, let me wear my fringed jacket and some jeans. Gee, Mom, today it's old *fashioned* to get dressed up—"

"You heard me." Meanwhile, there is bathroom commotion. You hear the arguments over tubs, over whose bath salts are whose. When you peer in, a perfumed steam nearly asphyxiates; bubbles are regurgitating all over the floor.

"Oh, dear, I didn't mean bubble baths," you moan. "Now you cannot sit and dawdle, there isn't time."

You scramble through drawers and closets to hasten the finding of sox, slips, hair-ribbons (thanking heaven they're still too young to resist). Less thankful when the fifth grader discovers there's a spot on her best pink velvet and you've got to fly to the rescue with cleaning fluid. "Though really, honey, you could just as well wear the outfit you wear to Sunday School. I mean you should dress nicely to go to the theatre, but it isn't like a party."

"How about you, Mom?" one of them challenges. "When're you getting ready? And what're you going to wear?"

"Well, I had my bath this afternoon. And I'm just not sure what I'm wearing yet."

The old dependable green plaid, you think. That's quick and simple. And you can dispense with the usual makeup job; after all it isn't as if you were going out with friends. Going with anybody important. . .

And then the shocked awareness hits. Anybody—*important?* Just your family, that's all. Just your children!

And they'll soon be adolescents—and kids get some weird ideas of appearance in their teens. If you're going to set them an example don't cop out now, Mom.

Resolutely you get your loveliest ensemble from the closet, your smart new dress shoes. Thank goodness you can skip the bath but not the glamor, not even the eye-makeup. You don your longest earrings.

"Hurry up," they're calling. "Hey, I thought this show starts at seven-thirty."

"Don't worry, I'm coming." Catching up bag and gloves you scurry down to join them. Your beautiful dressed up family, for whom you could do no less. And they regard you with appreciative eyes.

"Hey, Mother, you look great." A son holds your fur wrap, a daughter opens the door. "Know something?" another voice admits as you all pile into the car. "We didn't think you'd go to all that trouble just for us."

"Just for you? Don't be silly. Everybody wants to look his best when he's going to the theatre!"

THE GROWING THINGS

You slip hopefully out with the plants—pinks and baskets of pansies, and the little lacquer-green azaleas still in their waxy wrappings. The children still seem to be happily occupied with hide-and-go-seek. Surely, just this once, you can have a peaceful hour of gardening alone. But no sooner are you settled on your knees with trowel and bucket than they spy you and come running.

"Watcha doing? Oh, let me, let me!" Even the littlest announces, "Me help." And a child from an apartment house, somewhat wistfully, "I could do a good job for you, I like to set out flowers."

You're licked, you know, from the start. This frenzied affinity little folks have for flowers is akin to their love for rabbits and puppies and kittens and baby birds. To deny it, however inconvenient, would weigh heavily on your heart.

"All right, fine, if you'll all be very careful and put them just where I tell you to."

Resignedly you begin to break up the pansies into clumps, to separate the pinks. A boy is set to digging holes, a task of which he quickly tires; but another who's been teasing for a turn, snatches the digger, as he calls it, and hacks away.

Water is slopped. Pansies get dirt in their limp unprotesting bonnets. The pinks, thank goodness, can be divided and subdivided indefinitely and later rearranged. And before you even get to the azaleas, half your eager assistants have wearied of the effort and trailed away.

But the littlest still squats, worse luck, poking and patting and getting underfoot every time you try to move. "This be my garden, okay?" she asks. "This be my very own garden, and when the flowers bloom, why I'll pick them for you, Mommy, and for my dolls sometimes, and I'll water it every day!"

But eventually she too skips off, and you look up to find only one child from the neighboring apartment house still lingering. Somehow, in all the confusion, this rather shy little person has been overlooked. "Here." You hand over one of the small azaleas. "Where do you think this would look best?"

"You mean it? I can really help?" Her face is awed but shining. She holds it gingerly, then points to the very place you had in mind. Together you begin to dig, to talk. You have company the rest of the afternoon. And though a part of you recalls the hoped-for solitude, the rest of you agrees:

It's all right. This is the way it probably ought to be. The grown—and the growing things. The fresh little new plants to be cultivated, whether flowers or children. And in the total scheme of things which means the most? A plant—or the happiness and wonder of a child?

WHEN LOVE BRIMS OVER

Wow curious is love, parental love, and how unexpectedly, almost foolishly, it comes flooding. . . .

A daughter tramps into the cabin kitchen one morning, still puckered wth sleep, hair disheveled, an old blanket wound Indian fashion around her, and asks, mildly grinning, "Can I make my own pancakes for breakfast?"

And, still clutching the absurd blanket against some fancied chill, hair straggling from the washerwomanish bun skewered atop her head, she onehandedly messes, stirs, and spills, and trudges placidly to the porch table, beaming at you and announcing, "See? I did it. They're sorta burned but don't they smell good?"

And for no reason at all there is light in your life and warmth and wonder, and the sweet, sweet flooding. . . .

Or a son gets up early for a promised jaunt to a nearby neighboring town, and remembers that he has promised to dig you some fishing worms. "Gee, d'you suppose you and the kids could go dig them yourselves?" he reminds himself at the last minute. And though tempted to yield, a firmness of duty presses through your quick weak longing of love, and you say, "Nope, that's a man's job, really."

And, reluctant but uncomplaining, he changes clothes, gets out the boat, and clanks off to the island. You see the boat beached in the sun, know he is buried deep in the marshy woods, and there is no sound but the slap of water, birds singing, and a great consuming tenderness washes through you. You call out to that dimly sensed, digging figure, "C'mon, honey, you'll be late, that's enough."

And as he comes rowing back, blond, sunburned, and lifts out the battered bucket, saying, "I hope that'll hold you, you should catch plenty of bluegills," and goes streaking off up the rock steps to be on his way once more, your heart is arrested. Held. There is a startling grip of wonder within you. For no special reason your whole being is filled with love.

♥ ♥ ♥

HOPING

Thirteen-year-old who has been asked to submit an autobiography for an English class: "I guess I'm not a typical teen-ager. I don't talk on the telephone and I'm not boy-crazy, but next year I hope to be."

THE SKATING RINK

The skating rink? Oh, no!" you moan, for it's been a rough day. The last place you long to land is in one of those noisy dens of delinquency, you think. "But the skating rink's so much fun," your daughter's friends are clamoring. "You can skate, too, you'll love it." "I can hardly wait," you mutter to your mate. "Hand me a magazine. I can curl up in a corner someplace, maybe."

Feeling very much the sacrificial lamb, you drive an interminable distance, prepared only to endure. Then it happens—maybe it's the organ music, throbbing to the rafters of this clean air-conditioned cathedral. Maybe it's the muted rush of wheels or the nostalgic scent of the hot dogs. Anyway, excitement strikes, a giddy sense of joy. You turn in your spectator's ticket, and order skates instead.

Clop-clop-clop; you reel, stagger, clutch the back of seats. Thus playing safe, you circle the outer rim of the vast ellipse, where the girls—some timorously at first, others blandly swift—are skimming. "Oh, come on!" they encourage. "It's lots smoother out here."

Terrified, but determined, you inch into the joyously gliding throng. And with courage comes confidence, then delight. Skills you'd thought long vanished begin to return with the nudging insistence of the tunes the organist is playing. New ones. Old ones like "The Skaters Waltz" and "Wabash Blues." The sheer joy of motion claims you. This is like flying!

Whole families are skating together, dads waltzing gracefully with teenage daughters; mother leading eager, stumbling tots. Church groups are here, Scout troops, girls in perky costumes. Uniformed attendants glide about, encouraging beginners, offering instruction, managing games, contests, specials. At exhibition time the experts take the floor, couples who dance on wheels with all the grace and beauty of ballet.

A sense of wonder claims you—and dismay at what you've been missing. Today's rink is clean, well-managed, sound-hushed. No drinking, almost no smoking—there are even rules about appearance. How much better than drive-ins or other places parents worry about. Here there is light and music and laughter, and the thrill of sheer physical motion. All of it pleasantly but firmly supervised by people who seem to love life—and old-fashioned fun.

What's more, it's inexpensive, compared to most entertainment. Rent your skates and stay all evening. Or bring your own.

How's your headache, mother?" a daughter asks, soaring up. "This is the last number, it's time to go."

"What headache?" you ask. "Don't tell me it's over, I'm just getting started. When can we come again?"

COZY IS THE CABIN

It's fun to be a woman when. . .

You enter your summer cabin with the family on a brisk, bright winter evening.

The air inside is like an icebox, cold enough to set the teeth on edge, but scented with the bitter tang of old burned wood.

Heaters are plugged in, and their rosy coils begin to sing.

Boys are dispatched for wood. There is the brisk crack of kindling being chopped, the rumble of logs being dumped on the floor beside the fireplace, where your husband kneels to coax the first blaze.

Little flames lick the paper and the rustling dry twigs and leaves. Like strong red mouths they curl about the logs, and with a hungry roar of pleasure begin to devour them.

People are hungry too. Still bundled in your wraps, you flatten the hamburger into round pink patties that soon are sizzling on the stove. The tea-kettle for the coffee begins to chuckle and croon.

You draw the table up before the fire and fill the paper plates. Hamburger, beans and coffee have never tasted so good.

You scout out extra blankets for the bunks, and go around tucking shivering little ones in.

You and your husband turn out the lights and sit in the cozy cave-like glow of the fire. You hear the low cluck of its conversation, the scratch of branches on the roof, and the rushing skirts of the wind.

She is like a woman running from some unknown peril in the dark. You hear her footsteps crackling through the leaves, her low plaintive cry, and the sound of her knuckles tapping at the window as if pleading to come in.

♥ ♥ ♥

ONLY A MOTHER EXPECTS

Unpacking a lunchbox to find it filled with such horrendous warnings as, "Die, you dog!" "Get out of town before sunset!" and "Stop flerting with Nancy or the possy rides tonight.". . .

To get up before breakfast and pop corn for a school party. . .

To paint fire engines on a little boy's pants.

THOSE WONDERFUL TEENS

No times can try parental souls like their children's teens. The period is a literal change of life for the youngsters physically, and it changes the lives of mothers and dads as well.

Fearful of all the dire trouble that can overtake them after dark (drugs, crime, sex) we often set unenforceable curfews, then worry and cross-examine if a son is five minutes late from the church picnic.

Stricken before the prospect of having an illiterate on our hands, we beat a path to the school to confer with teachers, and lecture about homework and college loud and long.

Society loads the dice against us with its incessant glamorizing of obscenity and violence, then claims it's our fault if our kids "go wrong."

These little items, plus such daily miseries as sloppy dress, endless telephone conversations, smart cracks, mind-boggling, ear-splitting music, and a room that looks as if it'd been stirred with a stick, combine to make us long for some blessed vaccine that would simply inoculate them (or us) against this emotional disease of simply Growing Up.

But until some Dr. Salk comes along with such an antidote, we have no choice but to make the best of them. And the best, if you can relax enough to see it, can be a pretty wonderful thing. Actually, parents have a front row seat for the greatest show on earth—watching life's most exciting creatures emerging from the cocoon. Sitting so close, of course, we see the bad features. But we're in a position to open our eyes to the good, as well.

For instance: *Their humor.* Adolescents are wonderfully funny. If you're sufficiently relaxed and objective about them, their antics and comments are an endless source of entertainment. And I don't mean in the sense of laughing at them or making fun. Their stories are often witty and hilarious, however long-winded, if we just stop nagging long enough to listen.

Their confidence and independence. They can lick the world with one hand tied, and they don't want you telling them how. Outrageous though this may seem at times, it is actually a thrilling demonstration of how good a job you've done of weaning and strengthening them for the battle ahead.

Their courage and sense of adventure. This too can worry you sick—or enhance the tempo of otherwise dull days. Who but crazy kids would explore caves, tackle rapids, racket penniless around this country or Europe on foot or in old cars, and live to tell their exploits at the table? Who but the very young would fell such giants, enjoy such narrow escapes? Since we are powerless to prevent it, we might just as well wrest such pleasure from it as we can.

Their generosity. They live big, think big, talk big— and give big, both of their earnings and themselves. A boy who may have to borrow lunch money from her later, will blow his whole week's pay on flowers for his mother. A girl will spend her entire vacation making sports shirts for her dad and brothers.

Their ideals. They really care about the poor, enough to go out and work for them in the mountains and the ghettos. They start drives to help the stricken and the blind. They are fervent about ecology; they want to preserve this planet and make it a better place to live. Most of them are against war, but they would fight if they had to for what they consider right. Their ideas of love and marriage bear watching.

They're impractical and unrealistic a lot of the time, due to sheer inexperience. They're often too noisy, too virulent; we don't approve their methods and their ideas often shock parents (just as *our* methods and ideas shocked ours).

But teen-agers can be survived. They can even be enjoyed—if we just stop wringing our hands long enough to applaud.

♥ ♥ ♥

MY FAVORITE NEIGHBOR SAYS. . .

"When I see these painfully tidy house-holds where there is no clutter of toys, no dust, no papers strewn about, I sometimes get uncomfortable, thinking of the mess our teeming family strews in its wake. And then I wonder. Usually these places are childless, or the homes of young couples with babies not yet old enough to make a mess. And I wonder if maybe this other isn't like soil to a plant? Possessions, even clutter, furnish a kind of natural nourishment for a family. You almost have to have it to enable you to put down your roots and grow!"

PLANT, BELIEVE, AND DREAM

Dialogue with a reader:

"I'll never forget a piece you once wrote about planting flowers surrounded by children who all wanted to help. But one by one they dropped off except a dear little creature from an apartment house, who stayed by your side all afternoon. And I thought about that little thing and her dream of beauty, as well as the companionship, that was embodied in the act of planting things. I've thought about it so much.

"For people who plant seeds or set out bulbs in the fall do so with a vision. They don't see just the bare ground before them—they see that flower. All during the time of waiting, sometimes for weeks, or sometimes during the whole long cold winter, they are sustained by that vision and that dream. They are willing to invest their energy and their time in the cause of that dream because they see it so plainly, the loveliness ahead."

"It's a little bit the way it is with raising children, isn't it? I mean—the time and the work you put into them in the hope that—well, eventually someday they'll bloom!"

"Oh, my goodness yes. Just—hanging on, that's the main thing. Just not giving up the hope, often through a long cold wintry time that seems to hold very little promise, that one day they'll amount to something, you'll be proud. And usually this happens, they come through. The daughter who seemed so awkward and out of touch while she was growing up marries a marvelous man. The youngster who was failing in high school is on the dean's list in college, going on to graduate school.

"And looking at them, hearing the nice things people say about them, you remember the hard days that are past, the days when about all you could do was set them out in the sun and watch them grow and just—hang on! And you realize more than ever how important it is to keep sight of your dream."

♥ ♥ ♥

HAVE YOU EVER WONDERED WHY?

Though you have such a hard time getting them to pick up their clothes, wash the dishes or make their beds—you can't decide to paint. . . or set out bulbs or bake a cake. . . or roll out a pie. . . or use the sewing machine without every child under ten in the family climbing all over you wanting to help.

LONG ARMS—AND BIG LAPS

Motherhood, it is said, is an instinct that rouses protective passion. We are very much like animals, we women with children. We will sacrifice our own comfort and safety for them. We will shield and shelter them, fight like tigers, if need be, on their behalf.

Yet motherhood is also a universal emotion. In civilized society it does, or should, advance beyond this primitive, defensive, "Mine, my children," and encompass all children, no matter whose.

They troop to your house after school. Is your child any hungrier than the others? Either for that cookie and glass of milk—or for praise?

"I got a star on my spelling today!" a shy little girl whose mother works, will confide.

"You *did?* Why, that's wonderful. My goodness, won't your parents be proud of you tonight? And because it's so awfully long till then, you reach out—you want to—and give her a congratulatory hug.

Or your own youngster spends the night, as mine did recently, with a neighbor. And this good neighbor, who was whipping up pinafores for her two daughters, stayed up till midnight fashioning a third, so that their friend also could have one to wear to school the next day.

"She looked so wishful when she saw them, I just couldn't bear for her not to have one too—"

Or the telephone rings, and someone has

taken time to pass along a compliment she has heard about your son. These deeds, these generous words—how wonderfully good! How they demonstrate the true maternal spirit that reaches out beyond its own sheltered circle.

And the wonderful thing about it is that the more love we expend on children—all children—the more we are enriched.

Be kind to that little stranger at your door selling seeds. Hail that leggy kid down the street and tell him you're proud to know he's just won a scholarship. Seek out the parents of those who've done well in the school program and warm their hearts with your praise.

Little fires light up in our hearts when we do. The kind that comes from having long arms—and big laps.

SUMMER WINDS UP LIKE A RIBBON

How swiftly summer draws to a close. In the beginning, when children fling their school books down and dads and mothers consult maps, check camping gear, read letters from distant relatives pleading, "Come!" summer seems like a green and golden ribbon stretching endlessly ahead. Now you can do all the countless things you couldn't before—sleep late, go or stay depending on a husband's vacation or your mood.

But almost before you are well into it, someone seems to be winding up the ribbon. Little snatches of it seem to be vanishing under your very fingers, then faster and faster it flies, drawing you along. "Where is the summer *going?*" people exclaim to each other. And the children—mournfully if older, eagerly if beginners, "Why, it's almost time for school!"

As it is, you realize with a breathless sense of things crowding in upon you. Only a few more days at the beach or the mountains—or lolling in your own back yard—ration them carefully, enjoy them to the hilt. Yet even as you postpone the inevitable, your mind is busy with shopping lists, doctors to be seen for health certificates, registration dates. Like signal flags the first precocious bronze or scarlet leaves appear. Over the last emerald scrap of summer the long red shadow of the school house leans.

Yet it is with mixed emotions that a mother trades the values of summer for those of having the children back in school. Now at last a little order.

With everybody up at the same time again a reasonable routine can be established for the day... And with everybody out of the *house*—! Projects dimly flirted with during the dreamy days of summer can be excitingly embraced: Paint the kitchen. Slipcover the couch. Do those Yoga exercises. Write poetry.

Like Winnie the Pooh who sang, "Here I am in the dark alone, there's nobody here but me," she exults, "Here I am in the house alone." She too can "sing whatever she wants to sing, laugh whatever she wants to laugh." And she does, fervently and often literally, if only to break the silence of the house.

The lovely silence, the beautiful silence, yet the aching silence when a house is empty of children and the spool of summer has wound up its ribbon and gone.

ONLY A LITTLE GRAY KITTEN

You hear the screaming in the street and at once, not pausing to reason, are being propelled by fear and instinct through the door and down the steps. And as you run you realize, there is no mistaking it—this is the voice of your child.

"Fella, Fella, Fella!" She and a playmate are standing white-faced at the curb. Not bodily injured, your senses telegraph. Not bleeding. But frozen in an attitude of terror that can only be expressed in these wild and frenzied cries. For there at their feet he lies, limp and still, her kitten, struck down by a passing car.

Your husband, right behind you, gathers up the tiny body that so recently was frolicking with its mother, while you embrace and try to quiet the child. Already a small crowd has gathered, convinced that tragedy has struck. "What happened?" someone asks as you lead the still weeping child away. "It was only a cat," someone replies. "Only a little gray kitten."

The crowd disperses, faintly troubled, faintly bemused. You try to calm the almost prostrate child as you lead her into the house. You bathe her face with cool water, hold her close.

"You still have Tammy. She'll have more kittens, or we'll get you another one." But she refuses to be consoled. "Fella, Fella!" she moans.

And you think—only a cat. Only a little gray kitten? No. To a child a pet is like having a child of his own. He feeds and cares for it; he cleans up after it;

he trains it and loves it and knows very real concern for it. And when it meets with disaster, why should we belittle its loss? Her suffering at this moment is no less than mine would be if I lost a child. Quite literally, her agony is as great.

There is, of course, this difference. Mercifully, a child's grief and despair do not last long. Yet right now, right now she is undergoing grief that merits respect. It is a preview of adulthood. It is a sampling of what lies in store for each of us when we are grown.

And for just a moment you cannot bear it, that anyone so young and small and vulnerable should have to face other such trials, most of them without you, most of them alone. Yet grow up she must. And there is this comfort—with the growing comes the strength to bear them. Life itself, through experiences like this, will have prepared her.

But for now, for just right now, you hold her close.

GETTING THE KIDS TO HELP

A friend says parents should work out a child job exchange: "Your own are always so much more willing to help somebody else. And theirs are generally not only willing but often eager to help you."

This is true. Neighbor kids will volunteer to tackle jobs your own offspring won't touch.

While from friends come flattering, if mystifying reports: "Your Johnny is a treasure—I've never seen such ambition. He pitched in and helped me clean the attic. He even hauled out the trash."

Maybe this is because a duty is something to be put off as long as possible, and gotten out of if you can. While it's always noble to be a volunteer. Also because outsiders are more prone to be lavish with praise.

So saying, here are a few helpful hints gleaned from experienced parents, for getting work out of your own progeny:

1. Be definite. Don't generalize: "Why didn't you clean the bathroom the way you're supposed to? and your room's a mess, and just look at this closet. You never help around here." Instead, assign specific household chores to be performed, if possible, according to a schedule. Children respect a boss who is himself well organized and able firmly to convey what he wants.

2. Make a list. When such tasks are written down this definiteness is not only visible, but

challenging. This also gives the boy or girl the satisfaction of crossing them off, as accomplished.

3. Don't give the youngster all the inconsequential jobs—such as setting the table, or all the dirty
ones—such as cleaning up after you. Let him bake
the cake, get the whole meal. Let him do constructive
things where he can see the results, instead of always
the drudgery.

4. Don't scold and criticize. When suggestions
are necessary, be tactful.

5. Don't rush in and start doing the whole thing
over. This is disastrous to pride, and makes the young
aide feel, "What's the use?"

6. Be generous with your appreciation. Brag
about him as lavishly as if he were—well, the kid next
door.

TIME OFF

*Every busy mother needs a friendly
neighbor with whom she can operate a child
exchange. Each will then be able to enjoy an
occasional child-free shopping spree, a bridge
date, or a luncheon. To make it work, however, remember these things:*

*1. It should come about naturally be-
cause of mutual need.*

*2. Both mothers should genuinely like
and get along with each other.*

*3. Both mothers should genuinely like
and get along with the other's offspring.*

*4. The youngsters themselves should be
good friends.*

5. Don't keep score, no tit-for-tat.

*6. Each should feel free to say no if it
just isn't convenient sometime.*

EVERY CHILD CAN BE BEAUTIFUL

I have been told of a family whose pet dog was so impossibly unattractive that they laughingly dubbed it Ugly.

Yet after a time, sheer affection brought about a change of heart, and half-kiddingly at first, they began calling it Beautiful instead. "And curiously enough," says my friend, "a change took place. The dog actually *became* beautiful!"

This is not as surprising as it seems. For beauty is not only in the eyes of the beholder—it lies in that which is beheld. And often it is the love, the encouragement, the praise, the feeling of being regarded as lovely, that nurtures the bud of beauty that sleeps in the plainest of us.

Children particularly bask in the sunlight of encouragement and praise. They respond to it, thrive on it. Yet often, with the most valid if mistaken motives, parents destroy a child's self-confidence instead.

I once heard a mother send her teen-age daughter off to a dance with these admonitions, "Stand up straight, you look like an old plow-horse. Stop frowning like that, you look bad enough in those glasses without making it worse. But don't grin all over either —your braces will show. Honestly, it's no wonder the boys won't dance with you."

And when the door had closed after the unhappy victim—"She's at the awkward age right now, but she's going to be quite pretty when she outgrows it. One thing sure, she'll never be vain."

No, never vain, I thought with a slight shock. But how much better to risk a touch of vanity than this vigorous attack on the very potentials of prettiness now.

It has been said that every baby is beautiful in his mother's eyes. And this is fortunate. But how much more fortunate it would be if we held onto this first, no doubt prejudiced appraisal and expressed it more often to the boy or girl: "How pretty you are, how proud I am of you.". . . "Your eyes are lovely, dear, they just light up when you smile.".'.'. "You're a fine looking boy, honey, stand up tall and proud."

If correlated with common sense and the proper reminders of modesty and manners, such encouragement will never produce vain offspring.

Choose the best points of your youngster's appearance, and praise them. And if bad features he has, help him to overcome them or accept them as inconsequential. Above all, remember that beauty is largely a matter of the spirit, an attitude, a state of mind.

Every child can be beautiful—if someone loves him enough.

♥ ♥ ♥

THE SMALL FRY SAY

"I didn't get up on the wrong side of the bed this morning, Mother. I just got up on the wrong side of you!"

102

RISING TO THE OCCASION

Oh, dear, I know what this is," a neighbor said, the other day, rising to answer the telephone. "The principal of the high school wants to talk to us about Jim, and I dread it."

Then, halfway to the instrument, she turned and grinned: "Did you ever stop to think that being a mother means just one long string of rising to the occasions?"

Rising to the occasion.

A child is hurt. You are young and inexperienced, your head spins, and for an instant you don't know what to do. Then forces stronger than you are take over—you rush to the rescue. If it's serious you call the ambulance, get him to a hospital, notify people, and are calm and noble until the danger is passed. Then perhaps you collapse—but you have risen to the occasion.

The PTA makes you chairman of the annual bazaar. You feel bewildered, hopelessly inadequate, your potentials overestimated. Yet the phone begins to ring, committees coalesce, results begin to show— and you know it will be a success. You are rising to the occasion.

You are called upon to make a speech for a cause that's vital to your children. (A stoplight, a playground, a cafeteria.) You're scared. You don't know what to say. They are all better at this than you. "I can't do it!" you think. But somehow you do—and do it effectively, at that. You rise to the occasion.

103

You must entertain some VIPs from your husband's company. Or show their wives the city. Or go with him to a foreign country. You lack the aplomb, you think; you lack the clothes, the courage—and besides, you don't feel well. Yet you manage it all so smoothly nobody suspects. You rise to the occasion.

A son gets into trouble. The police call—it's actually happening to you. You don't see how you can face it, but you do. You rise to the occasion.

A daughter announces her engagement to a boy you scarcely know. You are startled and stricken, you want to prevent a foolish marriage at all costs, yet you want to do right by everyone. Filled with dread but determined, you contact the other family—who are just as stunned as you. You do what is expected of you, the wise and gracious thing.

The list of such challenges is endless. And being a parent means being in a state of constant preparation to meet them. The ability to put one's own comfort aside, one's own pride at times, one's own personal wishes, and go forth—perhaps quaking inside, but outwardly shoulders back, chin firm, head high. Rising—forever rising to the test with which life confronts us.

Rising to the occasion!

NO BOY SCOUTS TONIGHT

Children farmed out with friends, you and your husband set off for a weekend alone in the country. Your bags are amazingly light and so are your spirits.

There's nobody on your lap, nobody leaning over your shoulder. Nobody fighting, nobody listening to rock 'n' roll. Nobody whimpering, "Daddy, where's a filling station? I've got to stop."

When you do finally stop at Freddy's, the country store, without the usual crew to feed, you need only coffee cream, a pound of home-cured sausage. And when you reach the cabin, a blissful quiet reigns. You are spared issuing the usual orders about chores, the usual warnings.

The sun is a great golden flower trembling on the lake as you sit on the patio, unwinding from a hectic week. And when an avalanche of Boy Scouts descends on the cabin across the water, your sense of escape and personal solitude is enhanced. "Well, here's to their noble leader!" your husband toasts that gallant volunteer.

Their green uniforms and scarlet neckerchiefs splash color as they rush about, wild with enthusiasm. Their fragrant campfire whets your appetite. "Let's go to George's for dinner. Then you won't have to cook."

In his log cabin restaurant George, the genial host, leads you to a cozy table and personally lights the candle. You beam on other couples with their

children—the same fond looks you've so often re-
ceived from people who don't have to cope with yours.

"Steaks," you order, mad with this extravagant
freedom. "Your thickest steaks for two."

The stars are crisp as you return. The pine trees
sweeten the tingling air. Across the way the campfire
still glows scarlet, dancing in duplicate on the lake
below. Someone is playing a guitar, you hear voices
singing, shouting.

Let's go sit on the terrace," your husband suggests. "Listen to the kids for a while."

"Well—if you want to." You make fresh coffee
and carry it down. The cups are pleasantly hot in
your hands, your wraps feel good. A plume of smoke
rises white against the trees as someone douses the
fire. A bugle pierces the night with taps.

"Wonder where they're all going to sleep," your
husband ponders.

"Oh, in tents, sleeping bags probably."

"Yeah, but it's getting pretty cold."

"Maybe they'll use their sleeping bags in the
cabin."

"That cabin's too small for all those kids," he
worries. "And we've got lots of room—"

"See here, whatever you're thinking, stop it!"
you cry, snatching up the cups. "We came here to be
alone, remember? Not to entertain a whole Scout
troop!"

YOUR CHILDREN'S FRIENDS

One of the nicest parts of being a parent is getting to know your children's friends. All the merry, comical, rioting, sometimes exasperating little personalities who flock about the house and yard when they're small.

But even more rewarding, the special relationships that develop when they get older. The individuals who come to the house seeking the companionship of a son or a daughter, meanwhile having a meal with the family, or settling down for a visit with you while the offspring keeps them waiting.

Sometimes even paying you the tribute of dropping in to see how you're doing when they know your youngster is away.

There is Sally, who never comes home from college without ringing the bell and catching up on the family. There is Gracie, full of songs and wisecracks and incredible tales. There is Jane, who wants to write, and Diane, the dancer, both confiding their ambitions.

There is Allen, sober, gentle, handy with a fuse or a wrench, and willing to help you move a piece of furniture. There is George, who can be induced to sit down at the piano and play a rhapsody, then pull up a chair and philosophize about peace and war. There is Van, who can give you glimpses of what life is really like in Red China. . . All these youngsters and more—new friends, old friends, sometimes including friends' sweethearts—what a joy to watch their young lives shaping up. To listen to them, advise them when they ask it, worry about them a little—but bear no real responsibility for them.

To like and be liked by your children's friends—what a joy!

♥ ♥ ♥

DO MOTHERS EVER SLEEP?

"Do mothers sleep?" your little boy asks.
"Certainly, why?"
"Well, whenever anybody calls you in the night you always come."
Sleep—do mothers ever truly sleep? . ..
Surely sleep is the lightest blanket that a mother pulls over herself. And however deeply she burrows into its comfort, another self perches on the rim of consciousness, alert and on guard. Let a child cry out, cough, even kick off his covers and be cold and the signal is flashed. Like a fish striking for the fly, she darts to the surface without even considering. She's out of bed and down the hall, heading unerringly for the proper child.
"Yes," you smile, remembering how your mother would appear wih the same mystifying promptness out of the dark. "Mothers sleep too. But not very soundly."

THE FAMILY CLIPPING BUREAU

In addition to her many other roles (cook, laundress, nurse, counselor and justice of the peace) a mother usually serves as the Family Clipping Bureau.

Let anybody be compiling a report, notebook or speech, be in need of current events or pictures depicting the tribal rites of the Aztecs, he has only to ask Mother. For somewhere she has seen or cached away something he can use. "There was something in the paper about that last Friday—or was it Saturday?" And off she scurries to root it out. Or, "A pamphlet on that very subject came in the mail. Look in my bottom drawer."

A mother will not only haul out all her lovingly saved reference matter, if she can't find something she'll still be hot on the trail via calls to friends, relatives, travel bureaus and foreign embassies. In fact, once drawn into the cause of a report on Cambodia or even her husband's five minute Exchange Club talk, it's sometimes hard to turn her off.

But there is another kind of Family Clipping Service that a mother provides unsought. It is the real reason she clings to her magazines, or streaks after whoever's carrying off the old newspapers with, "Wait! I haven't gone through them yet."

I haven't gone through them yet... seeking what? A vaguely remembered article about a boy who put himself through college (for Jim). Or that psychologist's advice to girls (it might help Nancy). Or that story about the ponies of Chincoteague (for Jill).

There are moments of frustration. "I *know* I saw it—somewhere." Sometimes she admits defeat. But when a prize is located her triumph is sweet. "Hooray!" On those rare occasions when she can find her scissors she uses them; when she can't, loving fingers suffice. Often these papers rescued from couch, floor, or a long repose in the garage, are grubby, jelly-stained and slightly torn. No matter, so long as the message remains. The bits of humor, advice or inspiration that she is convinced will guide and brighten the life course of those dear to her.

Pleased, a mother delivers these offerings. That the response is not always madly enthusiastic doesn't faze her. Weeks later she may come upon her little gem lying where she left it. Or even in a wastebasket (the picture she thought Ginny might want to frame, the words that were to have been an inspiration). Happily, the typical clipping bureau mother isn't offended. Something tells her that her services are not entirely in vain.

Once, long after an older daughter had left on her honeymoon I came across a little essay on kindness she'd never mentioned nor even read, I thought, carefully copied in a composition book. While for years I carried a yellowed scrap of verse that my mother had planted somewhere in my growing up— and that I don't suppose I even thanked her for... these are the hidden rewards of a mother's clipping bureau.

WHEN IT'S TOO LATE
FOR SPILLED MILK

You think sometimes you can't stand it —the noise, the confusion, the demands: "Where's my gym suit?"... "I need some money."..."Take me, hurry, if I'm late I'll be kicked out of the band."

The telephone ringing, the fighting (dogs and cats and kids). The spilled milk, the broken china, the silver that goes down the drain. The things they borrow without asking. The accidents, the missed buses, the school conferences and warning notes. The emergencies—always on a day when you've got something important planned.

The high temperatures, physical and emotional. The egos that must be propped, the tempers that must be controlled. The hearts sometimes so shattered you wonder how you can help pick up the pieces and glue them together again.

And your children won't mind and won't *listen,* or take the advice you offer or that they implore you for. And it all seems so much trouble that you sometimes wonder how you ever got yourself into this. Even wonder if it's worth it. And secretly dream of the time when they'll be able to take themselves places, use their own things, solve their own problems, run their own lives. When you'll have a little peace and privacy in which to rediscover *yours.* (If there's enough energy left over, and there's still something worth finding, something that's survived.)

Then as they fly off one by one you begin to see it happening.

The complications thinning out, the gradual lessening of the clutter. The car is more often available, the telephone free. The house is not only more civilized, it's quieter. . . so much *quieter*. . . .

And along with the relief, a kind of shock assails you. You do a dazed retake. "So soon?" you think. "Hey, now, let me think this over. . . hey, wait!"

♥ ♥ ♥

MY NEIGHBOR SAYS

"The kids are all gone, and the house is so clean and quiet I yell sometimes and throw a little dirt around."

ENVY THE CHILDLESS?

Not long ago I read an article by a brisk, bright young married woman who announced that she and her husband 'intended to go through life childless.

Her reason being that she had viewed with a shudder "the unhappy creature who is mother first, wife second, woman third and human being last." She stated further the lengthy complaints she had heard from couples burdened and bowed by a family, and accused the majority of American mothers of being trapped malcontents leading lives so frustrated and unfulfilled that if the truth were known (and some of them admitted it) they envied her.

Well, maybe. Sometimes. But anyone with a modicum of sense knows that you can't list a woman's roles in the order given; you have to be a kind of package mix of woman-wife-mother-human being, and you're certainly a more vital personality for the combination.

Sure, we're weak and human. Sometimes, viewing the charmingly carefree, glamorous negligee, velvet sofa (without protective slipcovers) existence of the childless, we may have moments of rebellion. But for every one of our complaints we hear the fervent statements of bored and lonely women telling us how gladly they'd change places with us.

Envy the childless? Not really. Not over the

long haul. Not when you've gone through the profound experience of giving birth and hearing your baby cry... Not when you and your husband are excitedly uncrating a bicycle for a birthday surprise... Not on Christmas Eve... Not even when you worry about them, and fight about them sometimes, and stand together beside a hospital bed praying that your son will live.

This is the stuff of life, of human involvement, of pain and growth and maturing. It's tough, sure, but whoever said that anything of value in this world came cheap or easy? Or that marriage has to be one long joyride in the tunnel of love to have significance?

When we're tempted to envy the deliberately childless, we have only to look about us to be thankful we have kids. Nearly every neighborhood has its couple so far gone in selfishness that they chase children off their grass, appropriate stray balls, and sometimes, if only to relieve the dreary monotony of their days, they call the police.

Or they lavish their stunted affections on pets which they feed at the table and address in baby talk. Or they obsessively baby each other. And when they lose each other you see them wandering around in stores, or sitting on park benches. They have nobody else who needs and wants them, no tall successful sons to carry on the family business maybe, and the family name. No daughters to have them over for dinner or the holidays; no grandchildren to spoil and boast about. Carefree most of their lives, they find nobody really cares what happens to them.

Envy the intentionally childless? How could we?

GUM AT THE WEDDING

How not to cry at your daughter's wedding. . .

She is four years old and bright and perky and her name is Susette. Her big brown eyes sparkled when asked if she'd like to be the flower girl. She pranced about with delight, her long hair bouncing.

She was good as gold at the rehearsal, strewing imaginary petals with abandon and beaming on all the empty pews. She was lark-happy, too, trotting from store to store seeking new shoes and the little white gloves and proper dress.

The dress was found, old-fashioned beige lace, an incredibly happy match for the lace bonnet that had been her grandmother's. She must don the whole costume and pose and strut for admiring relatives.

But by the vital day she was tired of the whole business. She resisted the dress, refused the bonnet, vigorously rejected the little white gloves. Even the appearance of her tiny basket failed to appease. She would accept it and submit to the bonnet only on condition that planted among the daisies and rosebuds would be plenty of bubble gum.

Frantic, the principals agree. The organist is already playing, the soloist warming up, people are being ushered down the aisle.

"But we'll wait till later to chew it, honey," you beg.

None of that, she wants it *now*.

"They're ready for you, Mother," says a son.

She'll be okay."

So you take your place up front. And choke back the tears you'd sworn you would not shed. And turn with blind pride and emotion as the wedding march swells and the bridesmaids appear, so young, so lovely, so gay. And you are aware of the beautiful vision that is your daughter on her father's arm. While ahead of them trots a perky little figure, who pauses halfway down the aisle to turn and call back to them with a vigorous gesture, "Come *on!*"

Then the bonnet with its long streamers, the little lace dress and its wearer is skipping toward you, gaily strewing petals—and chewing gum.

Earnestly climbing the altar steps, she stands there beaming upon the congregation, jaws and fingers busy as she strives to produce a bubble worthy of the occasion. Failing, she drops the wad, stoops to retrieve it, brushes it off and pops it back in her mouth.

As you shake your head, she sweetly spits it out and pokes the bridesmaid, who is intent on the ceremony. The startled bridesmaid, not knowing what else to do with it, hastily sticks it under her bouquet...

The vows are almost over. The gladsome bells ring out, the radiant couple is rushing by...

So if you don't want to cry at the wedding, try a tiny flower girl with bubble gum.

THE SOUND OF CHILDREN

Some friends of ours visited a beautiful retirement village not long ago, and found it charming: "But we missed the children. Even when your own are grown it's fun to live in a neighborhood where you still see school buses stopping at the corner, and kids of all ages going by, junior and high school. It would seem so lonely without them"...

Yes, and little ones telling their mothers goodbye at the door and skipping off, often with their lunch boxes. And at night to hear the games kids still play outdoors, the shouting and the running. Sure they trample your flowers sometimes, and swing on your fences—but the big ones are handy for mowing your yard, and the little ones to play jacks on your steps, or just sit there petting your cat.

Children add life to a place—and to those who live in that place.

So it seems to me a little bit sad and sometimes mistaken when people who don't *have* to, move to a condominium in Florida or any community where they will have the sole company of adults. True, there are many situations where this is the only sensible decision. And true, too, that when the kids are younger and driving you crazy, such an ultimate fate looks like sheer heaven... But don't be too sure, and don't be too hasty.

We, too, recently spent a weekend with relatives in the midwest whose house once swarmed. Now, with all the empty rooms came a kind of emptiness upon us too. Without all the interruptions we used to have even the conversations seemed flat. And our shopping and sightseeing jaunts, though assuredly more peaceful, lacked flavor. Finally, our host exclaimed, "I know what's the matter, it's just too quiet around here, let's call in some neighbor kids!"

SHOE SHOPPING FOR TWO

A young mother writes: "How interesting things are with two! We went out to buy our two small daughters two pairs of shoes apiece. They took off four shoes and tried on eight, which were the wrong size, so they tried on eight more, which were the wrong style. That made 20 shoes scattered at odd points throughout the store because, of course, each new shoe had to be walked on and admired.

"Finally when we'd chosen the ones we wanted we had quite a time finding the ones they'd worn in, then the new shoes we were taking, and the mates in the right size. The trouble seemed to be the vast quantity of single shoes we were dealing with—in the neighborhood of 62.

"What would it be like to have three or four children to deal with, or five or six?

"But I think I'd enjoy leading five little girls into a shoe store to buy two pairs apiece just for the adventure.

"Would you ever find your way back to the shoes you started out with? How many clerks would you need? Would they ask the other customers to step aside? Would they refuse to wait on you?"

NO MATTER WHAT YOU CALL HER

*M*other.
"The sweetest name in the English language," my own mother used to say. True, she was a sentimentalist—but surely we have a right to be sentimental when it comes to mothers. The very word *Motherhood* has an emotional depth and significance few terms have. It bespeaks nourishment and safety and sheltering arms. It embraces not only the human state but the animal kingdom— the tiger fiercely protective of her cubs, the hen clucking over her brood and spreading her wings to shield them from the storm. It speaks of the very beginnings of life in egg or womb, and of nurture in the most critical stages thereafter.

Mama is a dear term too, connoting very little folks new to language. "Mama" is easy to say, and its call from the crib usually brings instant attention... Some people, especially in the south, cling to the diminutive "Mama" all their lives. And there is something very appealing about this, suggesting submission and loving dependency, despite the evidence of years. I personally find it somehow touching to hear a strong responsible man still referring to his mother as "Mama."

Ma is very old-fashioned. It is locked curiously into the hardships of the pioneers. Blunt, raw, a trifle sad, yet filled with a humble dignity. This word too stirs up tenderness in me, for my grand-mother was one of those brave women who lost

119

babies in a sod hut on an Iowa prairie. Her tall sons called her "Ma" all their lives, and no word was ever spoken with more devotion and respect; nor could any word hold more love than that word "Ma" on my grandfather's lips.

Mom has been modern now for years. It is casual, comradely. It says that a child regards his mother as a friend as well as sometimes an enemy. Yelled or fretted, called out kiddingly or in anger or distress, into that single syllable is packed a whole way of life. The parent-child relationship is simply different than it used to be. Modern mothers don't represent as much authority, and we spend less time with our children. We have so many interests, they have so many interests. We often see each other on the run between activities. "Mom" has surfaced as a kind of tumbleweed word for an often frantic, continually changing role. Yet it too signifies an affection, a tie, a depth that is totally at odds with its seeming casualness.

Mother... Mama... Mom... Whatever your sons and daughters call you (or you call your own) any woman who has ever had children knows that the mind to worry about them, the lap to hold them, the arms to hug them are the same. (Yes, and the feet that rush to their rescue.) And that long after they've outgrown your lap and the pressing against you to measure their height—your heart still feels that pressure.

No matter how big they grow or how far from you they wander, they will always be just one size: As tall as your heart.